Conte

C000004932

INTRODUCTION

WALK

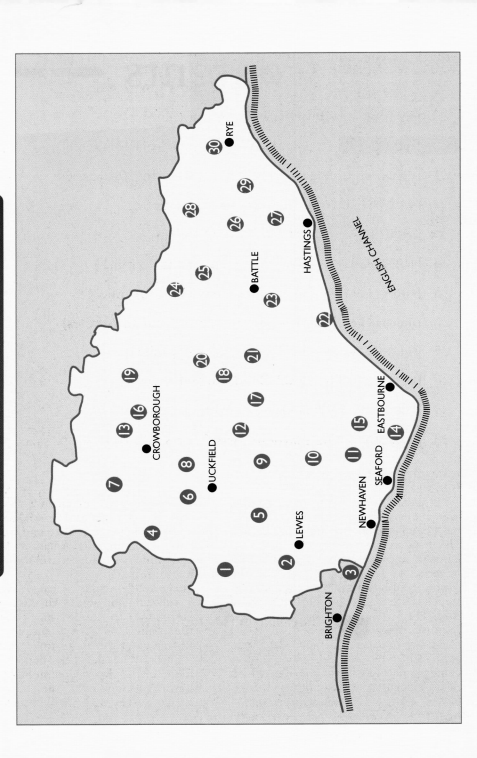

AREA MAP SHOWING LOCATION OF THE WALKS

PUBLISHER'S NOTE

We hope that you obtain considerable enjoyment from this book; great care has been taken in its preparation. However, changes of landlord and actual closures are sadly not uncommon. Likewise, although at the time of publication all routes followed public rights of way or permitted paths, diversion orders can be made and permissions withdrawn.

We cannot, of course, be held responsible for such diversion orders and any inaccuracies in the text which result from these or any other changes to the routes nor any damage which might result from walkers trespassing on private property. We are anxious though that all details covering the walks and the pubs are kept up to date and would therefore welcome information from readers which would be relevant to future editions.

The sketch maps accompanying each walk are not always to scale and are intended to guide you to the starting point and give a simple but accurate idea of the route to be taken. For those who like the benefit of detailed maps, we recommend that you arm yourself with the relevant Ordnance Survey map in the Explorer series.

Much of East Sussex is still remarkably quiet and unspoilt. Thankfully, two extensive areas are partially protected by designation as Areas of Outstanding Natural Beauty (AONBs).

To the south, a wide swathe of the South Downs between the county boundary to the north of Brighton and the high chalk cliffs at Beachy Head above Eastbourne lies within the Sussex Downs AONB, now earmarked for additional protection as part of a new National Park. For the best of downland walking try Walks 3, 11 or 14.

To the north, much of the 560 square miles of the High Weald AONB is within East Sussex, a surprisingly thinly populated area of great variety and beauty, embracing the open heathland of Ashdown Forest (Walks 6 and 7), the river valleys formed by tributaries of the Eastern Rother and the Upper Medway as well as areas of ancient and planted woodland, small scale agriculture and a sprinkling of villages and small towns, many of them beautifully situated, high on the so called 'forest ridges' which extend across the county between Heathfield and Hastings.

The walks included in this book are classified as strolls and all are short, varying between 2 and $4\frac{1}{2}$ miles in length. Although most of the routes follow clear, well maintained paths and are easy to follow, some, in the depths of the High Weald, are little used and can become overgrown, particularly when crops are at their height and weeds flourish in late summer. I have indicated the potential trouble spots in my route descriptions and would recommend setting out armed with a stick to deal with any encroaching nettles or brambles, particularly between July and September.

Also, be sure to have a map to hand in case you do go astray, preferably the appropriate OS Explorer sheet noted for each walk.

In selecting the pubs on which each of the walks are based, I have tried to avoid those which have featured in previous volumes of pub walks published by Countryside Books. This means that several well known and popular pubs are missing from this collection. It *doesn't* mean, however, that those chosen are, in any sense, hostelries from the 'second division'. All offer a warm welcome to walkers, several are family owned and run, and most would qualify for the label, spotted recently on the door of a pub in Lancashire: 'This is a pub that serves good food, not a restaurant that sells beer.' In spite of this distinction, the choice of pub food on offer is extensive and varied, embracing such specialities as Thai cuisine, authentic curries, top quality pizzas and a wide range of vegetarian dishes though, quite rightly, most of the pubs featured in this book still concentrate on native fare, notably a wide variety of pies, almost invariably prepared on the premises from local ingredients.

All but one of the walks in this book start and finish at the featured pub, where you can park in the pub car park, ideally letting the landlord know that you are there and with the obvious proviso that you also patronise the pub.

As always it has been a great pleasure putting together a collection of walks, seeking out remote and often unfamiliar country pubs and exploring a landscape of great richness and variety. I hope you can share this pleasure by following in my footsteps.

Ben Perkins

Wivelsfield Green
The Cock Inn

MAP: OS EXPLORER 122 (GR 354200)	**WALK 1**	**DISTANCE:** $3^3/_4$ MILES

DIRECTIONS TO START: FROM THE B2112 DITCHLING TO HAYWARDS HEATH ROAD TURN RIGHT BY BALDOCK'S GARAGE. THE COCK INN IS ON THE LEFT AFTER JUST UNDER A MILE. **PARKING:** YOU ARE WELCOME TO PARK IN THE PUB CAR PARK WHILE ON THE WALK.

Although never far from the built up area of Wivelsfield and Wivelsfield Green this walk, encircling the village, remains surprisingly rural. It offers a variety of features including two ancient trackways, probably once used to transfer stock between summer and winter grazing, mature mixed woodland, hay meadows, parkland and a charming 13th to 15th century church. You will be walking on the sticky clay of the Low Weald so be prepared for some mud underfoot, particularly along the tracks used near the start of the walk which double as bridleways and can get badly churned up in places.

The Cock Inn

The Cock Inn has been a pub since at least 1835 and, although never an official coaching inn, was used as a stopover for coaches and riders on the old London to Brighton road which passed nearby. The interior, although extensively rearranged in recent years, retains the traditional public and saloon bars. The old stable and tack room next door has been converted into a single storey dining room. Outside there is a brick patio at the front and a small garden. The pub has a resident ghost in the form of a white lady, seen so far only by a psychic customer though the owners have experienced unexplained manifestations such as suddenly opened windows, lights switched on and off and screams in the night.

The Cock is a free house, family owned and managed, offering good home-made food from an extensive menu with many traditional bar snacks and main dishes plus some less usual extras including a range of authentic curries. Harveys Sussex Ale plus two regularly changed guest beers are on hand pump and connoisseurs of the hard stuff have a choice of 50 single malt whiskies. Well behaved children and dogs are welcome. Opening times are 11 am to 3 pm and 6 pm to 11.30 pm Monday to Saturday and from 12 noon to 3.30 pm and 6 pm to 10.30 pm on Sundays. Telephone: 01444 471668.

The Walk

① From the pub turn left and, after a few yards, go right along Downsview Drive.

Turn left on a path which starts between houses number 17 and 19 and go forward along the left and right edge of successive areas of rough pasture to join a track. Turn right and follow this shady tree-lined track southwards for 500 yards to join a road.

② Turn left and, after 30 yards, go right along another clear unmade track which soon opens out to follow a right field edge. Follow the track on through woodland and out via an access drive to join a road. Turn right.

③ After a little over 100 yards go left over a stile and follow a winding, occasionally waymarked, path through West Wood, ignoring several side and crossing paths. Drop down gently, soon walking parallel to the northern wood edge. Cross a gully and, after a few yards, turn right, leave the

PLACES OF INTEREST NEARBY

About a mile to the south along the B2112, the **Ditchling Common Country Park** is a pleasant place for a picnic and a chance to explore the 200 acres of open heath and grassland, embracing a variety of natural habitats.

Wivelsfield church

wood and follow a hedge to join a lane. Turn left.

④ Just past a pair of cottages on the right, labelled 'Hope Cottages 1868', turn right along a signed path, enclosed at first, then along the right edge of two meadows with a footbridge between them. At the second field corner you will come to a stile. Don't cross it. Instead, turn squarely left within the same field and follow a fence to a gate. Continue through two fields and two more gates out to the B2112. Cross the road and turn right beside it.

⑤ After 100 yards, just short of Baldock's Garage, go left along a drive. Skirt to the left of a bungalow, cross a concrete bridge and bear right to a stile. Go ahead across two fields, in the second field converging on the hedge to your left. Go through a squeeze stile in this hedge and bear right, soon with Wivelsfield churchyard on your left. From the field corner a short enclosed path leads out to a lane. Turn right, follow this lane out to the B2112 and turn right again.

⑥ After 200 yards go left over a stile, forward beside a fence to a gate and along a farm track. Shortly side step to the left through a squeeze stile and resume your previous direction beside a fence, on across the next field to a stile, across a lawn and along a house drive to a road.

⑦ Follow the drive to Wivelsfield Hall, opposite. After a few yards go right through a kissing gate. Cross the middle of a field to a stile in the field corner and go across the next field, walking parallel to power lines. Skirt to the right of a protruding hedge corner and pass obliquely under power lines to a stile. Keep to the right and left edge of successive fields out to join a road through a builder's yard. Turn left back to the pub.

Plumpton
The Half Moon

MAP: OS EXPLORER 122
(GR 363132)

WALK 2

DISTANCE: 3 MILES

DIRECTIONS TO START: PLUMPTON IS ON THE B2116 WHICH RUNS ALONG THE FOOT OF THE DOWNS BETWEEN DITCHLING AND THE A275 NORTH OF LEWES. **PARKING:** YOU ARE WELCOME TO USE THE PUB CAR PARK WHILE ON THE WALK, BUT LET THEM KNOW FIRST.

This is an exceptional walk which samples two of the magnificent, centuries-old terraced paths or bostals which are such a characteristic feature of the northern escarpment of the South Downs. From the pub our walk loops northwards along field paths before tackling the strenuous but well graded climb through patchy woodland up and out onto an open National Trust area of close cropped downland pasture at the top of the scarp slope. It is worth the effort. From the trig point on the 675 ft summit of Blackcap, crowned by a maturing tree clump, the view is one of the finest in the county; eastwards along the ridge of the Downs to Firle Beacon, south towards the sea through the Ouse gap and northwards across a wide Wealden panorama backed by the distant heights of Ashdown Forest.

The Half Moon

Dating from the mid-19th century, the Half Moon was once a staging post for horse-drawn coaches. Perfectly situated at the foot of the Downs, it is now a popular dining pub for tourists and families out for the day from Brighton and can get very busy at summer weekends. The traditionally decorated bar has an open fire with a games room at one end and a cosy raised dining area at the other. Outside, on the patio, the rustic wooden tables are shaded with trellises entwined with wisteria and clematis. At the rear is a large lawn with tables and an inventive children's play area. The menu is a substantial one, mostly home made. Try the macaroni cheese with crusty bread or homity pie, more of a flan really, made from potato, cheese and bacon. Also on offer are a range of individually named ploughman's such as the Footpad's Platter (brie, smoked salmon and prawns) and an assortment of savoury or sweet pancakes. The two beers on hand pump are Harveys Sussex and Fuller's London Pride. The opening hours are 11 am to 3 pm and 6 pm to 11 pm on weekdays and all day at the weekend during the summer. Dogs must be on a lead and children are welcome, except in the bar. Telephone: 01273 890253.

The Walk

① Start the walk northwards from the pub along Plumpton Lane. Shortly fork right through a gate and go ahead across a meadow, soon with a high flint wall on

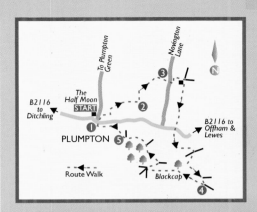

your right. Go over a stile, cross a drive and veer half-left across a field to join and go ahead along a headland track with a wood on your left.

② Follow the track as it bears squarely left. After about 150 yards cross the drive from Odintune Place and veer half-right across a field. Go over a stile about 30 yards to the right of the far field corner, cross another drive and stile and follow a left field edge out to a lane. Turn left.

③ After 60 yards, just past a brick cottage on your right, turn right along a farm track laid with concrete strips. Just past the last farm building at Warningore Farm on your right, turn right along another track and head for the Downs, continuing over a low summit to the B2116. Follow the track

PLACES OF INTEREST NEARBY

The village of **Ditchling**, to the west along the B2116, is well worth a visit, with many old houses and an interesting local museum. High on the Downs to the south of Ditchling are the twin mills of **Jack and Jill**, two of the most distinctive landmarks on the South Downs. Access is from the A273. Jill, the restored white post mill, is open on Sunday afternoons in the summer.

The view from Blackcap

opposite which soon climbs steadily between high wooded banks. About half way up the hill go straight over a crossing track and follow a narrower path.

④ At the top of the hill where you come out onto an open area of pasture, turn right at a waypost and walk up to the summit of Blackcap. Continue past the trig point and down to a gate. Don't go through the gate. Instead, just short of it, turn right on a track which soon begins to descend between grassy banks. After about 200 yards, at a waypost, double back to the left along a sunken bostal

path. For the first few yards walk along the bank to the right of the path from which you get a fine bird's eye view of the earlier part of the walk. About half way down the hill, at another waypost, keep left (almost straight on).

⑤ Where the main track bears round to the right, turn left at a waypost. Leave the woodland over a stile and drop diagonally down across the middle of two fields. At the B2116 turn left along a segregated path to the left of the road. Carry on beside the road for the short distance back to the start.

Rottingdean
The Plough Inn

MAP: OS EXPLORER 122
(GR 369024 – PUB; GR 371021 – START)

WALK 3

DISTANCE: 4 MILES

DIRECTIONS TO START: ROTTINGDEAN IS ON THE A259 COAST ROAD ABOUT 5 MILES EAST OF BRIGHTON. **PARKING:** PARK IN THE MARINE CLIFF CAR PARK (FEE PAYABLE) ON THE SEAWARD SIDE OF THE A259 ABOUT 100 YARDS EAST OF THE TRAFFIC LIGHTS AT THE JUNCTION OF THE A259 AND ROTTINGDEAN HIGH STREET (B2123). THE PUB HAS NO CAR PARK.

Although lost to East Sussex following its recent absorption into the Brighton and Hove Unitary Authority area, I have not let this fact deter me from including the charming village of Rottingdean in this collection of walks. From a starting point high on the cliff top, our walk follows the High Street to reach the oldest quarter of the village where the church and the Plough Inn face each other across the village pond and green. Nearby are The Grange, once the home of the artist Sir William Nicholson, now the public library; The Elms, occupied briefly by Rudyard Kipling; and North End House, once the home of another artist, Sir Edward Burne-Jones. Our walk takes us over the Downs to Ovingdean before turning towards the sea. The return route follows the top of the high chalk cliffs back to the start.

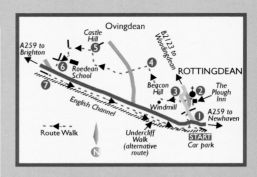

The Plough Inn

Occupying a prime position overlooking the village pond, the Plough Inn is a fairly modern building, though traditionally designed and blending well with the surrounding elegance. The interior consists of a large bar and adjoining dining area with a restaurant upstairs, open at weekends. There is a small walled patio at the rear but no garden or car park. The Plough is a Bass-owned pub serving, as might be expected, Bass on draught plus the locally ubiquitous Harveys Sussex Bitter. The food menu, too, is one that is common to all Bass houses, but offers a fair variety, including sausage and mash and a 'Mexican Fajita Feast'. You can also choose from the usual bar snacks, sandwiches (cold or toasted) or filled jacket potatoes. Children are welcome in the dining room and dogs in the bar.

Opening times are 11 am to 11 pm Monday to Saturday, 12 noon to 10.30 pm on Sunday and food is served daily from 12 noon to 2.30 pm and 6.30 pm to 9.30 pm. Telephone: 01273 390391.

The Walk

① From the entrance to the Marine Cliff car park, turn left, walk down to the traffic lights and go right along Rottingdean High Street. Take the second turning to the right (Vicarage Lane) and follow it round to the left past the Plough Inn and the village pond on the left.

② Opposite the church entrance on your right, turn left along the right edge of the village green, leaving The Elms, the home of Rudyard Kipling at the beginning of the last century, and the entrance to Kipling's Garden on your right. Join another road and turn right.

③ After less than 100 yards go left along a rough track, signed as a public bridleway, which narrows to a path and climbs steadily up and out onto the grassy ridge of Beacon Hill. At the top, with Rottingdean Windmill away to your left, turn right along the ridge, following a clear path which passes, on the left, a stone plinth marking the site of the various beacons which have been lit here over the last 400 years.

④ At the edge of the built up area of Ovingdean, turn left and drop downhill along an estate road with houses to your right. At the bottom of the hill cross a road (Greenways) and the stile, opposite, and climb along the right and left edge of two

PLACES OF INTEREST NEARBY

The **Grange Museum** is housed in an elegant Georgian building opposite the Plough Inn. It contains regularly changed exhibitions of local interest and the work of Sussex artists. Opening hours are weekdays 10 am to 4 pm, Sundays 2 pm to 4 pm. Telephone: 01273 301004.

Rottingdean's village pond and green

successive fields. Soon after the path levels out, ignore two stiles, instead turning right, along the left edge of the same field.

⑤ In the field corner, just short of a gate, go left over a stile and ahead along a right field edge, over the highest point of Castle Hill. Continue down the right edge of the next field. Towards the bottom of the hill, go over a stile and turn left along a path which follows the foot of a bank, rising up to your left, and then curves right out to join a road.

⑥ Turn left in front of the main entrance to Roedean School and forward along the left edge of an open grassy area. Bear right along the access from a car park, cross the main coast road near its junction with Roedean Road and walk out to the edge of the cliff.

⑦ Turn left and follow the cliff edge path back to Rottingdean. About half way back, steps allow access down to the beach and the undercliff walk which provides an alternative route in good weather.

Chelwood Common
The Coach and Horses

<table>
<tr><td>MAP: OS EXPLORER 135
(GR 411286)</td><td>WALK 4</td><td>DISTANCE: 2½ MILES</td></tr>
</table>

DIRECTIONS TO START: FROM THE A275 LEWES TO EAST GRINSTEAD ROAD AT DANEHILL, JUST NORTH OF THE PO/STORES, FORK RIGHT, SIGNPOSTED TO CHELWOOD COMMON. THE PUB IS ABOUT A MILE ALONG THIS ROAD. **PARKING:** PATRONS ARE WELCOME TO PARK IN THE PUB CAR PARK WHILE ON THE WALK.

The fringes of Ashdown Forest provide some of the most attractive walking in Sussex. Patches of heath and woodland, remnants of the original forest, are interspersed with small areas of farmland. The valley between Chelwood Common and Danehill explored on this walk also contains quite a few upmarket residences but most of them are well hidden by trees and make little impact on the rural quality of the area. Although fairly up and down, none of the climbs are long. Two tiny iron-coloured streams, both flowing southwards to form the River Ouse, are crossed and recrossed during the walk and offer particular charm and delight.

The Coach and Horses

Beautifully situated on the lower slopes of a quiet valley this solid sandstone building, originally a small Victorian alehouse, has now been expanded into a spacious but completely unspoilt pub, a free house in private ownership. The open plan interior is divided into three cosy bar areas on three levels, with wood or brick floors and open fires or wood burning stoves. At one end is a dining area, converted from a single storey stable block. Outside there is a large beautifully kept garden and an informal play area for children. The beers on hand pump are Harveys Sussex Bitter plus a regularly changed guest beer. For food, you can choose from some unusual and interesting bar snacks such as grilled Welsh rarebit ciabatta, an open sandwich with blue brie, bacon and lettuce or a ploughman's featuring Sussex Scrumpy Cheese made with cider, herbs and garlic. The ploughman's and ciabattas are not available on Sundays but there is also a substantial main menu boosted by blackboard specials, available every day. The puddings look particularly delicious. How about an Eton Mess (crushed meringue and strawberries folded with whipped cream)?

Opening hours are 11 am to 3 pm and 6 pm to 11 pm, Monday to Saturday; 12 noon to 3 pm and 7 pm to 10.30 pm on Sunday (weekend daytime opening may vary). Children and dogs are welcome. Telephone: 01825 740369.

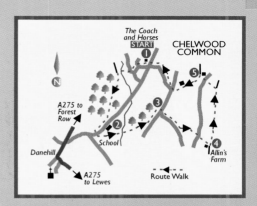

The Walk

① From the crossroads by the pub, start the walk along a narrow lane, signposted as Coach and Horses Lane, leaving the pub on your right. At a T-junction turn right and after 50 yards turn left along the left edge of the forecourt of a house called Kiln Wood. A narrow path continues down into a valley. Cross a footbridge to the left of a pond and turn left. Shortly, where the path divides, keep left along a clear path at the foot of a wooded slope. Go straight over a signposted crossing path and shortly go forward along a drive for a little over 100 yards before forking right along a narrow path. After 5 yards, where the path divides again, keep left. Ignoring side paths, follow the main path as it contours along the hillside and finally converges on a lane.

PLACES OF INTEREST NEARBY

A mile south of Danehill on the A275 is **Heaven Farm**. The buildings, dating from 1830, house a museum, incorporating barns, stables, piggeries and an oast house. There is also a tearoom. From the farm, a 1½ mile nature trail takes you through ancient woodland, notable for bluebells in spring. Telephone: 01825 790226.

Charming sandstone cottages near the pub

② Bear right along the lane. Just past Danehill School on the left and about 10 yards short of the road junction with Collingford Lane, turn sharply back to the left along a rough track which narrows to a path. Go straight across the access drive to a house called Pepper Alley on your right, cross a footbridge and climb. A path takes you past two more houses and steadily up through an area of patchy wood and heath, then forward along a gravel drive to a lane where you should bear left (almost straight ahead).

③ At a road junction turn right, signposted to Brookhouse Bottom. After about 250 yards, just short of the gateway to a house called Rough Acre on the left, turn left along a grassy path which skirts to the left of a landscaped garden. Cross a paddock, go over two stiles in quick succession and veer slightly right, dropping down across rough pasture to the next stile, soon in sight. Cross a footbridge and go ahead, climbing fairly steeply through thick woodland.

④ At the top of the hill, at a T-junction by a house (Allin's Farm), turn left along a lovely old enclosed path between tree-lined banks. After 650 yards turn left over a stile and head slightly right across a field, dropping down to another stile. Go over a footbridge in a wooded dip and climb across a lawn to join the drive from a large sandstone house.

⑤ Turn left and follow the drive out to the lane. Go right and immediately left along another narrow lane which takes you back to the start.

Isfield
The Laughing Fish

MAP: OS EXPLORER 123 (GR 451171)

WALK 5

DISTANCE: $2^1/_2$ MILES

DIRECTIONS TO START: ISFIELD IS SIGNPOSTED FROM THE A26 LEWES TO UCKFIELD ROAD ABOUT 5 MILES NORTH OF LEWES. THE PUB IS JUST TO THE WEST OF THE RESTORED ISFIELD STATION. **PARKING:** IN THE PUB CAR PARK WITH PERMISSION

Isfield is a small village in the Ouse valley north of Lewes and the highlight of our walk is a mile or so along one of the most attractive river banks in Sussex. Lined by trees and without 'improvements' such as raised embankments, the river meanders naturally through lush water meadows over which you can wander freely, thanks to a Countryside Stewardship agreement. This not only allows open access at least until 2006 but also ensures that these rich pastures are farmed organically. The main riverside path is a right of way and permanently open. The only potential problem is a tendency for the whole area to flood at times during the winter months. About half way round the walk you will come to the isolated but busy Anchor Inn which not only offers another opportunity for refreshment but also has rowing boats for hire during the summer months.

The Laughing Fish

Built as a railway hotel next to Isfield station in the 1920s, it became a pub only after the Uckfield to Tunbridge Wells line closed in 1969. It is a now a quiet, unpretentious and friendly village local, trading under the Greene King banner, and is an ideal pub for walkers. The spacious plainly furnished bar is decorated with various fish themed pictures and ornaments. Outside are a shady garden and a well-equipped children's play area. The beers on hand pump are Greene King IPA, Harveys Sussex Bitter plus one or two guest beers from the Greene King range such as Abbot Ale. The food on offer includes a particularly wide range of snacks, including club sandwiches and jacket potatoes with a generous choice of fillings. The main menu embraces many old favourites plus a choice of nine authentic Indian curries and some blackboard specials such as home-made fish and prawn pie.

The opening hours are 12 noon to 4 pm and 7 pm to 10.30 pm all the year round, extended to all day on summer weekends. Food is available from 12 noon to 2 pm and 7 pm to 9 pm. Children and dogs are welcome. Telephone: 01825 750349.

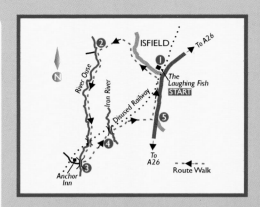

The Walk

① From the pub turn right along the road. After about 400 yards, just before the road bends to the right, turn left along the metalled access drive to Old Mill Cottages, signposted as a public bridleway. Follow this drive past the house entrance on the left after where it dwindles to a track.

② Just short of a bridge over the River Ouse (White Bridge) turn left over a stile and follow the left bank of the river. After the first field you will enter a Countryside Stewardship area, embracing several large water meadows sandwiched between the Ouse and the Iron River, at one time the main waterway. After leaving the Stewardship area walk under the old railway track and continue beside a more open stretch of river bank.

③ When you are opposite the Anchor Inn on the other side of the river and just short of a bridge across the Ouse providing access to the pub, you should turn sharply back to the left within the same field. Walk parallel to the meandering right field edge with a high hedge on your right.

PLACES OF INTEREST NEARBY

The former Isfield railway station, next to the Laughing Fish, has been lovingly restored along with ¾ mile of railway track to the north. Operating as the **Lavender Line** it runs steam hauled trips at weekends during the summer months. Telephone: 01825 750515.

The delightful River Ouse

④ At the far end of this field go over a footbridge and forward across a smaller meadow to cross a wider farm bridge over the Iron River. Go ahead across two more fields with a stile between them, walking parallel to a fence and the track bed of the old railway away to your left. At the far end of the field go over a stile half hidden behind a large oak tree and forward along a left field edge to join a lane through a wicket-gate.

⑤ Turn left. After a little over $1/4$ mile, at a road junction, turn left over the level crossing next to Isfield station, for the last few yards back to the pub.

Fairwarp
The Foresters Arms

| MAP: OS EXPLORER 135 (GR 468265) | WALK 6 | DISTANCE: 3½ MILES |

DIRECTIONS TO START: FROM THE NORTHERN END OF THE UCKFIELD BYPASS, FOLLOW THE B2026 HARTFIELD ROAD NORTHWARDS. FAIRWARP AND THE PUB ARE SIGNPOSTED ALONG AN UNCLASSIFIED ROAD TO THE RIGHT AFTER ABOUT A MILE.
PARKING: YOU ARE WELCOME TO PARK IN THE PUB CAR PARK WHILE ON THE WALK.

The walk, mostly along broad forest rides or tracks, starts through patchy woodland to the north of the pub. We are then quickly out onto the more open heathland to the west of the B2026 where a steady climb takes us up on to higher ground with sweeping views southwards to the Downs. Much of this heathland is now being managed by grazing and cutting to control the bracken and restore large areas of heather, which has already returned sufficiently to offer an impressive display during the summer months, approaching point 4. Although the walk description starts and finishes at the pub, the 'Hollies' car park at point 4 provides an alternative starting point, allowing you to visit the pub half way round the walk. The Duddleswell Tearooms are also within easy reach of the described circuit.

The Foresters Arms

This 100 year old pub enjoys a perfect setting opposite the village green and backing onto the woods and heathland of Ashdown Forest. Previously owned by King and Barnes of Horsham, it is now a Badger pub. The large central bar has a timber-beamed ceiling and leads into a dining area with a large wood burning stove. At the rear is a sheltered garden, filled with flowers in the summer months. The beers are Badger Best, Tanglefoot and Golden Champion. The long wine list features a 'wine of the month', available by the glass. The extensive menu kicks off with a long list of tempting starters followed by an à la carte choice embracing a variety of steaks and home-made pies, augmented by blackboard specials. To round the meal off you can choose from at least a dozen mouth-watering puddings. For those with more modest appetites the bar snack menu is equally comprehensive.

The opening hours are on Monday to Saturday from 11 am to 3 pm and 6 pm to 11 pm and on Sunday from 12 noon to 3 pm and 7 pm to 10.30 pm. Food is served daily from 12 noon to 2.30 pm and 7.30 to 9.30 pm. Children and dogs are equally welcome. Telephone: 01825 712808.

The Walk

① From the pub turn right and, after about 250 yards, just beyond the end of the village green on your left, turn right along a gravel track, waymarked as part of the Maresfield Millennium footpath.

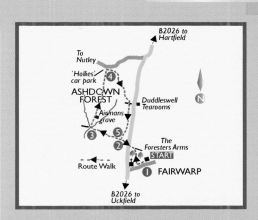

After about 100 yards, where the Millennium path forks left, keep right (almost straight ahead) with the main track. Where the track bears round to the right you should go ahead along a narrow path, now back on the Millennium walk, which skirts to the right of Fairwarp churchyard. Where you have a choice of paths, keep right with the main path. Go straight over a crossing path. At a wide crossing track where there is another Millennium path waypost, turn left and walk out to the B2026 road. Cross the road and continue along the access drive to Spring Garden Farm, opposite. Almost immediately, just past a cattle grid, fork right along a forest track.

② At a wide crossing ride, where the Millennium walk goes off to the right, you should go ahead, still on a broad track and heading generally westwards. Where you have a choice of three paths ahead, take

PLACES OF INTEREST NEARBY
Two miles to the west, **Nutley Windmill**, a restored open trestle post mill, is open on the last Sunday of every month and Summer Bank Holidays, 2.30 pm to 5 pm.

The Airman's Grave passed on the walk

the one in the middle (almost straight ahead), soon beginning to drop down.

③ At the bottom of the hill, where there are two footbridges, cross the first of these only before bearing half-right on a track which climbs steadily up, soon out on the open forest. You will pass a small enclosure, known as the Airman's Grave, containing a simple cross commemorating the crew of a Wellington bomber which crashed near here in 1941. Continue steadily up for over ¹/₂ mile.

④ On reaching the 'Hollies' parking area on your left and about 40 yards short of a road, turn right along another wide forest ride. Soon a wide panoramic view opens out southwards to the Downs. Where the

ride divides, keep right (almost straight on). The track now contours along the upper slope of a valley which drops away to your right. Go straight across a metalled drive, now back on the waymarked Maresfield Millennium walk (for the Duddleswell Tearooms go left along the drive to the road and left again, returning the same way). Follow the main ride as it drops gently down for 600 yards. Ignore side paths and walk straight across another metalled drive.

⑤ On reaching a crossing ride you will find yourself back at point 2. Turn left with the Millennium walk and retrace your outgoing route back across the B2026, on for 150 paces, then right back past Fairwarp church to the start.

Friar's Gate
The Half Moon Inn

MAP: OS EXPLORER 135
(GR 498334)

WALK 7

DISTANCE: $2^3/_4$ MILES

DIRECTIONS TO START: FRIAR'S GATE IS ON THE B2188 WHICH LINKS THE B2026 ON THE TOP OF ASHDOWN FOREST WITH GROOMBRIDGE IN THE MEDWAY VALLEY TO THE NORTH. THE HALF MOON PUB IS ON THE EAST SIDE OF THE ROAD ABOUT 4 MILES SOUTH OF GROOMBRIDGE. **PARKING:** THE PUB HAS A LARGE CAR PARK WHICH YOU MAY USE WITH PERMISSION WHILE ON THE WALK.

Friar's Gate, as the name implies, was once one of the hatches or gateways in the pale surrounding the Royal Hunting Forest of *Asshes Doune*, established in 1268. The highlight of this exceptional walk is a traverse across an extensive tract of open access land which is still part of Ashdown Forest, though detached from the main bulk of this 6,400 acre area of mixed heath and woodland, now in public ownership.

The earlier part of the walk involves a steady climb up through the privately owned Five Hundred Acre Wood, an attractive and well managed area of mixed woodland, incorporating ancient oak and beech, scattered conifers, patches of chestnut coppice and a few more open areas of bracken and silver birch. There is also much new planting, partly to replace trees destroyed in the Great Gale of 1987.

The Half Moon Inn

After a period of closure, the Half Moon, refurbished with care to avoid any loss of the traditional pub atmosphere, is now open and flourishing. It gets particularly busy during the warm summer months when patrons spill out from the single spacious L-shaped bar area into the sheltered front garden with tables shaded by colourful umbrellas and across the large back lawn with adjoining bandstand and children's play area. The food menu is a varied and mostly traditional one, ranging from simple bar snacks to substantial main dishes, but also including a choice of 'authentic' Indian curries. The core menu is supplemented by a Sunday roast and blackboard specials. The beers regularly available on hand pump are Harveys Sussex and Fuller's London Pride as well as Guinness on draft.

Opening hours are 12 noon to 3 pm and 6 pm to 11 pm Monday to Friday, all day at the weekend. Telephone: 01892 661270.

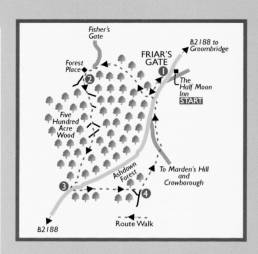

called Forest Place on the right, fork left along a roughly metalled track which climbs steadily up through the wood. Where you have a choice of tracks ahead keep to the one on the left, signed as a public path. Where the track divides again, this time into three, yours is the middle one. Shortly go straight over an oblique crossing path and continue to climb steadily. After $2/3$ mile, beyond a gate, bear right along a track which, after about 100 yards, converges on the B2188.

The Walk

① From the pub walk south beside the B2188 taking care as it carries fast traffic and has no verge. After about 200 yards turn right along a metalled drive, signed as a private road but also as a public footpath. It passes through an extensively replanted area within the northern edge of Five Hundred Acre Wood.

② After about $1/2$ mile, where the drive divides, fork left. Just beyond a house

PLACES OF INTEREST NEARBY

The famous **Pooh Sticks Bridge**, known to all children, has recently been rebuilt. It is marked on the Explorer map and is actually within practicable walking distance as a detour from our described circuit ($1/4$ miles each way from point 2). By car you must drive north via Withyham and Hartfield to reach it, parking at GR 470332 for a $1/4$ mile walk each way. Take your own Pooh Sticks as the whole area around the bridge has been scoured clean of stray twigs.

Five Hundred Acre Wood

③ Cross the road and follow the marked horse track opposite which heads out across the open access land of Ashdown Forest as a track not marked on OS maps. The trees thin to give fine views across the valley to Marden's Hill and the wooded heights on the edge of Crowborough. The path now drops down across more open heathland. Where it divides keep left with the main path.

④ After 100 yards turn left along a more substantial track which takes a level course, contouring along the gentle slope, and brings you out to a road. Turn left and at a junction with the B2188, go right back to the start.

High Hurstwood
The Maypole

MAP: OS EXPLORER 135 (GR 494256)	WALK 8	DISTANCE: 3 MILES

DIRECTIONS TO START: HIGH HURSTWOOD IS SIGNPOSTED NORTHWARDS FROM THE A272 BETWEEN MARESFIELD AND BUXTED, NORTH OF UCKFIELD. ALTERNATIVE ACCESS IS POSSIBLE ALONG A NARROW LANE EASTWARDS FROM THE A26 UCKFIELD TO TUNBRIDGE WELLS ROAD. **PARKING:** IN THE PUB CAR PARK WITH PERMISSION.

High Hurstwood is a scattered community, well off the beaten track, tucked down in a secluded valley on the eastern flank of Ashdown Forest and accessible only along narrow lanes. The walk follows several tracks, probably of ancient origin, lined by high banks and shaded by trees, making this a good walk for a hot summer's day. The last part of the circuit follows a fine and more open section of the Vanguard Way, a long distance path en route to the coast at Seaford having started, somewhat improbably, from East Croydon. The paths are mostly well signed and easy to follow but you may encounter some mud underfoot, particularly beyond point 3 where the track has been eroded by timber hauling operations. Towards the end of the walk you will pass an odd but engaging church, largely Victorian, with a partially timber-framed clock tower and separate belfry.

The Maypole

The present pub was built in 1871 to replace a former coaching inn which was housed in what is now known as Maypole Farm, a lovely timber-framed building dating from the 15th century, just about visible from the road through gaps in a high hedge almost opposite the pub. The 'new' Maypole Inn comprises an L-shaped open plan bar in traditional style with a separate poolroom. Outside is a patio and large garden. The beers presently on offer include the popular Harveys Sussex Ale and Courage Directors. The traditional and very competitively priced pub menu includes all the usual bar snacks as well as home made delights such as shepherd's pie and beef stew with dumplings, supplemented by a Sunday roast during the autumn and winter months.

The pub is open Monday to Thursday from 11 am to 3.30 pm and 6 pm to 11 pm, and all day on Friday, Saturday and Sunday. Food is available from 12 noon to 2 pm and 6 pm to 9.30 pm. Children and dogs are welcome. Telephone: 01825 732257.

The Walk

① From the pub turn right (north) along the road, passing the recreation ground and village sign on the right. Shortly turn left along Perrymans Lane. After another 200 yards or so, cross a stream and immediately fork left along a concrete drive. Where the drive ends go ahead along a narrow path within a strip of woodland. Where your forward progress is barred by a fence and an aggressive notice

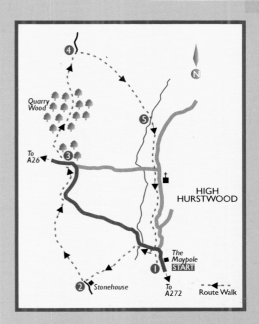

'No right of way, beware large dogs', turn right up steps to a stile and then left along a field edge. In the field corner go over a stile, right for 5 yards only and then, just short of a gate, left along a grassy strip between hedge and fence.

② Go over a stile and down steps to join a wide track and turn right to follow it uphill between high tree-lined banks. A few yards beyond the point where the track opens out on your left go forward over a broken stile to the right of a gate and follow a right field edge. The right of way, although partially waymarked, is a

PLACES OF INTEREST NEARBY

Wilderness Wood, about five miles away along the A272 at Hadlow Down, east of Buxted, is 60 acres of working woodland, with laid out trails, play areas, an exhibition, tearooms and shop. Telephone: 01825 830509.

The view to High Hurstwood

little vague as it passes to the left of two small stable blocks, using a gate and a gap between staggered rails to join a drive which takes you out to a lane. Bear left along the lane (almost straight ahead). Follow the lane as it rounds a left-hand bend, ignoring a stile on your right unless you would like a short cut back to High Hurstwood.

③ After another 150 yards fork right through a gate and along a deeply rutted tree-lined track. A clear path continues through Quarry Wood where side tracks should be ignored. Leave the wood over a stile and go forward along a right field edge.

④ After 400 yards turn right up steps in a bank and head out across high ground, now on the Vanguard Way where a fine view opens out towards the South Downs. On the other side of the field go ahead, beginning to drop down with a hedge on your right until you can go right over a stile in this hedge. Follow a trodden path obliquely down across a meadow. Join a fence on your left and follow it on down into the valley. A path continues between fence and hedge.

⑤ At the bottom of the hill cross a substantial footbridge over an iron-coloured stream. Shortly go forward along the gravel access drive from a cottage, following it out to a lane. Bear right along it for a little over $1/2$ mile back to the start.

East Hoathly
The Foresters Arms

MAP: OS EXPLORER 123 (GR 520161)

WALK 9

DISTANCE: $3\frac{1}{4}$ MILES

DIRECTIONS TO START: EAST HOATHLY IS SIGNPOSTED FROM A ROUNDABOUT ON THE A22 EASTBOURNE TO UCKFIELD ROAD ABOUT $\frac{1}{2}$ MILE EAST OF HALLAND. **PARKING:** PARK IN THE PUB CAR PARK OR THE FREE VILLAGE CAR PARK BEHIND THE PUB, NEXT TO THE CHURCH.

Sandwiched between the Downs and the High Weald, both protected as designated Areas of Outstanding Natural Beauty, the flat or gently undulating landscape of the Low Weald is often unjustly neglected by walkers. Now intensively farmed, the area was once heavily wooded. The name of the village is derived from the Old English *hodleigh*, meaning heather-covered clearing and, as also reflected in the name of our featured pub, East Hoathly was once at the centre of a flourishing forestry and woodworking industry. The walk, although mostly along field paths, passes through and around Great Wood which once lived up to its name but has now been reduced to a modest size, even smaller than as marked on the latest OS maps. A word of caution, the path beyond point 4 may be overgrown and awkward to follow, particularly in high summer. As an alternative, carry on along the lane into East Hoathly.

The Foresters Arms

The Foresters Arms is housed in a building largely unchanged since the late 17th century and is one of the longest established of the 44 pubs in the ownership of Harveys of Lewes. This independent brewery, founded in 1790 and still family owned and run, supplies many of the pubs featured in this volume. The pub has all the attributes of a welcoming village local – a simple beamed interior divided along traditional lines into saloon and public bars with wooden tables and bench seating and an open fire in the main bar. There is a small dining area at one end and a garden at the rear. The main beer on hand pump is, as might be expected, Harveys Sussex Bitter, supplemented by rotating seasonal ales from the same source. The food, all home cooked, is a cut above the average. The main menu includes such enticing dishes as confit of duck or rack of lamb with rosemary and redcurrant sauce and you can choose from some unusual snacks and starters including vegetarian offerings such as baguettes with houmous and cucumber crudités or a panier of spinach and goats' cheese.

The pub is open all day, every day, from 12 noon to 11 pm and food is served from 12 noon to 2 pm and 7 pm to 9 pm. Dogs and children are welcome. Telephone: 01825 840208.

The Walk

① Start the walk through East Hoathly churchyard, behind the pub. A path continues to the right of the village

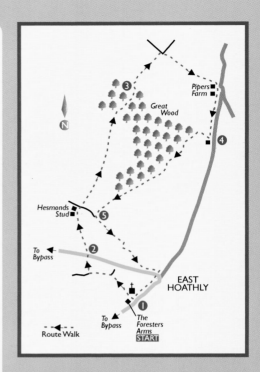

school. Where the tarmac path bears right, go ahead along a narrow path (if overgrown there is an alternative in the field to the left). Continue along a left field edge, go through a gap in the field corner and immediately turn right to follow a right field edge out to a road.

② Cross the road and follow the drive opposite. Go ahead past the buildings at Hesmonds Stud and forward along a

PLACES OF INTEREST NEARBY

About 4 miles to the west the **Bentley Wildfowl and Motor Museum** provides an ideal family outing, with picnic areas, shop and tearoom as well as vintage vehicles and some rare wildfowl including black swans and flamingos. It is open daily from April to September, weekends only in winter. Telephone: 01825 840573.

The start of the walk

weatherboarded Well Cottage, turn right along a narrow path. Once out into a field the right of way officially veers half-left across the field aiming for a segment of distant downland, visible between trees. If obstructed by crops, follow the right field edge round. Go through a gap about 5 yards to the left of the far field corner and continue along a meandering right field edge with a wood on your right (the official path again takes a straight line parallel to the field edge but may be blocked by crops). Continue along the right edge of two more fields, still with a wood on the right. Go through a wicket gate about 10 yards to the left of the second field corner and follow the right edge of the next field, passing a cottage on your right.

grassy strip to the left of a concrete drive. Where the drive ends, go ahead, climbing gently with a hedge on your right and a post and rail fence on your left, signposted as the Wealdway. Where the path opens out go ahead, passing to the right of the graves of two horses and forward on a wide path through Great Wood.

③ Leave the wood over a stile and go ahead, veering slightly left to another stile and on across another field. Cross a footbridge and go forward to a solitary tree. On reaching this oak tree, where the Wealdway goes off to the left, turn squarely right to a stile in the hedge. Continue along a field edge and then a farm drive out to a lane. Turn right and immediately fork right, signposted to East Hoathly.

④ After ¼ mile, just short of the white

⑤ Just short of a brick garden wall, turn squarely left across a field to a stile, on through a belt of woodland and then right, following a post and rail fence round two sides of a paddock. About 60 yards beyond the first field corner, go right over a wide sleeper bridge, squeeze through wooden railings (no stile) and go half-left across a paddock to join a road. Turn left back into East Hoathly.

Ripe
The Lamb Inn

MAP: OS EXPLORER 123 (GR 510101)	**WALK 10**	DISTANCE: 2 MILES

DIRECTIONS TO START: RIPE CAN BE APPROACHED NORTHWARDS FROM THE A27 LEWES TO EASTBOURNE ROAD AT SELMESTON OR SOUTHWARDS FROM THE B2124 AT LAUGHTON.
PARKING: IN THE PUB CAR PARK WITH PERMISSION IF ALSO PATRONISING THE PUB.

The focus of this walk is the charming village of Ripe. Although small and remotely situated in the middle of a thinly populated area of flat arable farmland, it still sustains a village shop as well as the flourishing Lamb Inn. This short walk follows little used field paths and quiet lanes to link Ripe with the nearby village of Chalvington, within the same parish, where you will pass a charming little 13th century church with weatherboarded bell tower and shingled spire. The return route passes the much larger church at Ripe where over the tower door is carved the Pelham Buckle, emblem of a once influential family which adorns many buildings in the area. The path out of Ripe can become overgrown during the summer months so it might be helpful to have a stick with you to beat down any encroaching nettles.

The Lamb Inn

Originally farmworkers' cottages and also once, in part, both village hall and bakery, the Lamb Inn is a now a friendly local of distinctive character with a large sheltered garden at the back. It is a free house in private ownership with an interior divided into small cosy areas and snug alcoves with wood panelled walls, beamed ceilings and pew style bench seating. The beer on hand pump is Harveys Sussex Bitter plus two regularly changed guest ales such as Marston's Pedigree or Fuller's London Pride. Five house wines are available by the glass. The main food menu is a large one supplemented by blackboard specials and includes some unusual dishes such as Sussex Smokie (smoked haddock in white wine, cheese and mustard sauce) and Dublin Pie (steak and mushrooms cooked in Guinness).

Opening hours are 11 am to 3 pm and 6 pm to 11 pm on Monday to Friday, all day on Saturday and Sunday. Children and dogs are welcome. Telephone: 01323 811280.

The Walk

① From the roundabout in the centre of the village, opposite the pub, follow the lane signposted to Chalvington and Berwick station, leaving the village shop on your left and the pub on your right. After a few yards, just past the parish notice board on your right, turn right along a roughly metalled access drive. You will pass on your right a white weatherboarded cottage with a blue plaque commemorating the short stay here of

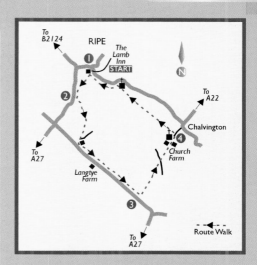

the novelist Malcolm Lowry. Where the drive ends go ahead along a narrow path which starts between two house entrances and heads south, overgrown in places. At a concrete drive go right out to a lane and turn left.

② After about 40 yards go left over a plank bridge and stile and ahead along a rough track. After another 60 yards go over a stile to the left of a gateway and veer half-right across a large field, passing immediately to the right of a wooden power pole. The path is liable to ploughing but one should be visible. In

PLACES OF INTEREST NEARBY

Two stately homes, both open to the public at certain times during the summer months, are within easy reach. **Glynde Place,** the home of Lord Hampden, dates from 1569 with later additions. **Firle Place** is the country seat of the Gage family, a Tudor mansion to which a Georgian façade was added in about 1740. For details of opening times telephone: 01273 858224 (Glynde) or 01273 858335 (Firle).

The 13th century church at Chalvington

the field corner go over two stiles and follow the direction of a yellow arrow on the second stile across a meadow to find a gate in the far left corner. Go forward across a garden to join a road through the access gateway from a cottage and turn left.

③ After a little over ¹/₂ mile along this quiet lane (Langtye Lane), lined by high hedges and some new tree planting, turn left through a gateway and go ahead along a right field edge where there are signs of use by horses. Chalvington church is soon in sight directly ahead. Go through a gap about 10 yards to the left of the field corner and resume your previous direction

along the right edge of the next field where there is a clear headland track. Continue between the buildings at Church Farm.

④ Turn left through an iron gate into Chalvington churchyard, pass to the right of the church and on through a similar gate. Go ahead along the right edge of a paddock to a stile and keep to the right edge of the field beyond. Continue across a field, currently used for turf cutting. A stiled and gated path crosses two small paddocks and then passes along the edge of Ripe churchyard and out via the church access to join a lane. Bear left along the lane back to the start.

Berwick
The Cricketers Arms

MAP: OS EXPLORER 123
(GR 519052)

WALK 11

DISTANCE: $3\frac{1}{2}$ MILES

DIRECTIONS TO START: THE VILLAGE OF BERWICK IS SIGNPOSTED TO THE SOUTH OF THE A27 LEWES TO EASTBOURNE ROAD WEST OF POLEGATE. THE CRICKETERS ARMS IS A FEW YARDS ALONG THIS LANE ON THE RIGHT. **PARKING:** YOU MAY USE THE PUB CAR PARK WITH PERMISSION.

The delightful village of Berwick, like many downland settlements, has grown up on the spring line at the foot of the northern downland escarpment where water bubbles up from under the chalk. Our walk heads for the Downs and soon commences a steady well-graded climb, using one of the many ancient terraced paths or bostals which are such a characteristic feature of the northern slopes of the Downs. Towards the top views open up, eastwards across the Cuckmere valley to Windover Hill above Wilmington, westwards along the line of the Downs to Firle Beacon and, from the summit, along the river valley to Cuckmere Haven and the sea. Above all, to the north you can enjoy the vast panorama of the Weald. The return route crosses fields and comes back past Berwick church, notable for some modern wall paintings by Vanessa Bell and Duncan Grant, members of the Bloomsbury Group (see Places of Interest).

The Cricketers Arms

Like the Foresters Arms at East Hoathly (Walk 9), the Cricketers Arms is one of the original pubs acquired by Harveys of Lewes and is still owned by the brewery. It is housed in a lovely old brick and flint cottage and consists of three simple rooms, two with tiled floors and open log fires and furnished with tables of scrubbed pine and high backed bench seats along the walls. In summer you can sit out in one of the colourful flower filled gardens at the front and rear of the pub. The Harveys Best Bitter and a changing range of Harveys seasonal ales are drawn straight from the barrel in the back room or you can choose from a generous selection of wines by the glass. The home cooked menu includes a particularly wide choice of seafood, as well as speciality sausages, a vegetarian dish of the day and the usual range of bar snacks.

Opening hours are Monday to Friday from 11 am to 3 pm and 6 pm to 11 pm, on Saturday from 11 am to 11 pm and on Sunday from 12 noon to 10.30 pm. Food is available daily from 12 noon to 2.15 pm and 6.15 pm to 9 pm. Children and dogs are welcome. Telephone: 01323 870469.

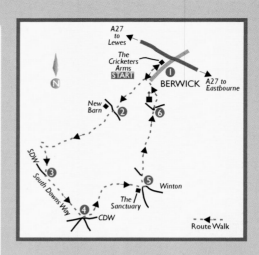

The Walk

① From the pub turn right along the lane. At a Y-junction turn right again and, shortly, where you have a choice of two concrete farm tracks ahead, fork left. Soon you are out in the open and heading for the Downs.

② At a T-junction with another track turn right and after 15 yards go left along a hedged path which heads for the Downs once more and eventually opens out and continues along the foot of a grassy bank rising up to your left. From the foot of the steepest part of the Downs escarpment, a terraced bostal path zigzags right and left up to the summit of the scarp slope.

③ At the top of the hill go forward between widely spaced fences to join a track and turn left, now on the South Downs Way which follows the ridge,

PLACES OF INTEREST NEARBY

Charleston, about 2 miles west along the A27, was, from 1916, the home of Duncan Grant and Vanessa Bell and the meeting place for the artists and writers who became known as the Bloomsbury Group. It is open from the end of March to the end of October from Wednesday to Sunday, 2 pm to 6 pm. Telephone: 01323 811626. Also nearby is **Drusillas Park**, a popular tourist attraction, incorporating a small zoo, miniature railway and playground as well as a shop and tearooms. Telephone: 01323 870234.

Looking westwards towards Firle Beacon

unfenced, between two large fields. As you proceed, the village of Alfriston comes into view ahead.

④ After about 600 yards, at a meeting of six paths, turn squarely left. There is a choice of two parallel tracks and yours is the one on the left. This hollow way, surfaced with chalk and flint, now descends steadily. At the foot of the slope follow it round to the right.

⑤ When you are opposite a large house on the right called The Sanctuary, at the point where the track joins a lane, you should turn left along another track. After 60 yards or so fork right over a stile and go ahead along a gently undulating headland path with the spire of Berwick church intermittently in view directly ahead.

⑥ At a junction with a track just short of the church, bear right and, immediately fork left along a grassy path and left again through a wicket gate into the churchyard. Skirt to the right of the church, leave the churchyard down steps and turn right to follow the church access path past a small car park and out to join a lane. Turn right, retracing your outgoing route to the start.

Waldron
The Star Inn

<table>
<tr><td>MAP: OS EXPLORER 123
(GR 549192)</td><td>WALK 12</td><td>DISTANCE: 3 MILES</td></tr>
</table>

DIRECTIONS TO START: WALDRON CAN BE APPROACHED ALONG NARROW LANES FROM THE A267 TUNBRIDGE WELLS ROAD AT HORAM OR FROM CROSS IN HAND, WEST OF HEATHFIELD. **PARKING:** IN THE INN CAR PARK (WITH PERMISSION) OR ON THE ROAD WHERE THERE IS REASONABLE SPACE OPPOSITE THE PUB.

Approached along a complex network of quiet lanes, the village of Waldron occupies high ground, hidden amidst an area of patchy woodland and small fields, many with well preserved hedges, on the gentle southern slopes of the High Weald. The walk descends southwards from the village, passing through a pleasant area of mixed woodland where mature oak and beech contrast with areas of chestnut coppice and more open patches of bracken and young silver birch. The lane back to the village at the end of the walk burrows between high sandstone banks before opening out onto the village square next to the church, also built from sandstone, with a 15th century tower housing a fine peal of eight bells and, outside, a rare Saxon font, carved from a single piece of stone.

The Star Inn

The Star has been in business since 1620 and occupies a delightful site, facing onto the spacious square and war memorial at the centre of the village and just across the road from the church. It is a free house in private ownership and remains very much a traditional village local. The large open bar area, framed by solid oak beams, has an impressive open fireplace at one end, with a fire-back dating from 1694. At the rear a dining area opens out onto a large garden. The beer on offer is Harveys Sussex Ale plus draught Bass and regularly rotated guest ale. There is also an extensive wine list. The lunch menu, which will be of most interest to walkers, includes home cooked pies and pasta dishes as well as several vegetarian offerings such as leek and stilton bake. Lighter snacks are also available and you can round the meal off with a choice of speciality coffees. The opening hours are daily from 11 am (12 noon Sundays) to 2.30 pm and 6 pm to 11 pm. Food is available except on Sunday and Monday evenings. Dogs and children are welcome. Telephone: 01435 812495.

The Walk

① Start the walk through the main entrance to the churchyard. Make your way round behind the church where you will find a stile from which you should head out on a trodden path downhill across two fields with a stile between them. On the far side of the second field go through a gate and head squarely out across the field beyond, walking parallel to the right-hand edge and then joining it.

② In the next field corner go ahead along a clear woodland path. On reaching a wider track on a bend, turn right and, after 20 yards, left along a narrower path which crosses a stream and brings you out to the edge of the wood. Turn right along the right field edge. In the field corner go through a gap and veer slightly left, gently up across the next field. Go over a stile about 10 yards to the right of the top left field corner and ahead across the next field to join a lane over a stile. (If a crop obstructs, you may find it easier to skirt round the right field edge.)

PLACES OF INTEREST NEARBY

Selwyns Wood Nature Reserve, less than a mile north of Waldron (car park GR 552206) is a small 28-acre area of mixed woodland, rather similar to the woods explored on the walk, but actively managed by the Sussex Wildlife Trust to protect the wildlife and also harvest areas of sweet chestnut coppice.

The attractive pub garden

③ Turn left along this quiet lane. After about ½ mile, at a road junction, turn left again, signposted to Waldron and Horam. Cross a stream and, after another 100 yards, go left through a gate and forward on a headland path with a high hedge on your right.

④ In the field corner go over a stile beside a gate and ahead up across a field to another stile/gate combination providing access into a wood. A few yards inside the wood, where the path divides, keep right. A narrow well-trodden path continues through the wood, never far from the right wood edge, eventually entering an area of sweet chestnut coppice. Where the path divides again fork right for 5 yards to a stile which takes you out to a field corner.

⑤ Bear left along the left edge of two successive fields. About 60 yards into the second field, go left through a wide gap in the hedge and right, resuming your previous direction, now along a right field edge. Towards the field corner the path winds ahead through a rather overgrown weedy area to a stile and continues up across pasture, where there is a trodden path parallel to the right field edge, to reach the southern end of Waldron churchyard and a well placed seat.

⑥ From here, either join the lane through a gate, turn left and walk up between high sandstone banks back to the start; alternatively scale the low fence and walk back through the overgrown, atmospheric and slightly spooky churchyard.

Boarshead
The Boar's Head Inn

MAP: OS EXPLORER 135
(GR 535326)

WALK 13

DISTANCE: 3 MILES

DIRECTIONS TO START: BOARSHEAD IS ON THE A26 UCKFIELD TO TUNBRIDGE WELLS ROAD ABOUT 1 MILE NORTH OF CROWBOROUGH. THE BOAR'S HEAD INN IS SET BACK TO THE EAST OF THE MAIN ROAD AT THE SOUTHERN END OF A REDUNDANT LOOP OF THE OLD A26. **PARKING:** IN THE PUB CAR PARK (WITH PERMISSION) OR IN VARIOUS PLACES ALONG THE OLD A26, NOW A QUIET CUL-DE-SAC.

Deep in the heart of the High Weald, a long and beautiful valley opens out to the north of the busy hilltop town of Crowborough. Rising in thick woodland, twin streams flow along the fertile farmed valley floor flanked by well-wooded slopes, on course to join the River Medway near Groombridge. Our walk crosses and recrosses the upper end of this valley, following a varied route, down through a well-tended orchard, across pasture and arable fields and steadily up amidst delightful semi-natural woodland, a good spot for bluebells in the late spring. The return route along part of the Sussex Border Path uses two sunken tracks lined by high banks, a characteristic feature of this rich sandstone landscape.

The Boar's Head Inn

Occupying a prime position in the middle of exceptional walking country, this fine old pub, dating from 1636, is a popular watering hole for walkers and rambling groups. The spacious bar area with exposed beams and inglenook fireplace is complemented by two dining areas which open out at the back onto a sheltered patio garden from which you can enjoy a wide view eastwards towards Rotherfield. Beers on hand pump are currently Harveys Sussex Ale, Flowers IPA and Wadworth 6X. The extensive food menu includes a full range of bar snacks and is notable for a choice of home cooked pies such as steak and kidney and chicken and ham. The puddings on display in the cool cabinet included, when I was there, a delicious-looking pear and peach strudel and raspberry cheesecake. Well-behaved dogs are welcome in the bar but the pub does not have a children's licence so youngsters must be confined to the garden or restaurant area.

The pub is open from 11.30 am to 2.30 pm and 6 pm to 11 pm on Monday to Friday, 11.30 am to 3.30 pm and 6 pm to 11 pm on Saturday, and 12 noon to 3 pm and 7 pm to 10.30 pm on Sunday. Food is available daily except Sunday evening. Telephone: 01892 652412.

The Walk

① From the pub, walk back along the old road and left along the new access link out to the A26. Cross the main road, turn right and after a few yards go left through a

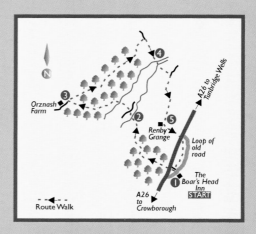

swing gate beside a large double gate. Follow a well-signed path forward through an orchard, then right as directed by a finger post. Shortly, at a path junction, turn left, descending along the right edge of the orchard to a stile and on down into a beautiful well-wooded valley.

② At the bottom of the hill go ahead over a wide culvert, forward up a low bank and then bear right along a right field edge. After 60 yards, at a four arm sign, ignore paths to right and left and head out across a large field, over a low summit and down to enter woodland over a stile. A few yards beyond a stream, at a path junction, bear left on a wider path along the valley and then steadily up. At a junction of four paths, go ahead, veering slightly left. Go straight over a wide crossing track and

PLACES OF INTEREST NEARBY

The gardens at **Groombridge Place**, a few miles to the north, have been developed as a major tourist attraction, with featured areas such as an 'enchanted forest', a 'drunken garden' and The Mad Hatter's Tea Room, all open daily during the summer. Telephone: 01892 863999.

Springtime in the woods around Boarshead

climb on a narrower path which brings you out to a wide farm track at the top of the hill.

③ Turn right. After a little over $^1/_2$ mile, just after the track bears round to the left at the corner of the wood, turn right along a signed headland path with a hedge, left. After about 150 yards turn right along a trodden crossing path which skirts to the right of an isolated tree clump and drops diagonally down across a field.

④ At the bottom, cross a stile and bear left along a hedged track which crosses a stream and climbs, soon between banks. At a T-junction turn right and follow another clear path which continues obliquely up the hill, soon once again between high sandstone banks. At the top you will emerge at a fine viewpoint.

⑤ Join a drive over a stile and bear right along it, past Renby Grange and out to the A26. Cross the road using the ramped paths provided and go forward along the redundant loop of the old A26 back to the start.

Exceat
The Golden Galleon

<table>
<tr><td>MAP: OS EXPLORER 123
(GR 513993)</td><td>WALK 14</td><td>DISTANCE: 3¾ MILES</td></tr>
</table>

DIRECTIONS TO START: EXCEAT IS ON THE A259 COAST ROAD BETWEEN SEAFORD AND EASTBOURNE. THE GOLDEN GALLEON IS NEXT TO EXCEAT BRIDGE IN THE CUCKMERE VALLEY. **PARKING:** YOU CAN PARK IN THE PUB CAR PARK WHILE ON THE WALK IF ALSO PATRONISING THE PUB.

The whole of this walk is within the Seven Sisters Country Park which covers 700 acres of cliff top and river valley along the glorious Heritage Coast between Seaford and Eastbourne. The Park was purchased by East Sussex County Council in 1971 at a time when it was being overwhelmed by cars and caravans. It is now managed by the Sussex Downs Conservation Board as a Site of Special Scientific Interest and a recreation area over which the public are free to wander more or less anywhere. Before setting out, it might be helpful to arm yourself with a leaflet, available at the Visitor Centre, marking the main features and the paths within the Country Park. Our described walk starts out along the Cuckmere River valley before climbing up onto the first of the Seven Sisters, an exceptional viewpoint. The return route offers an optional climb over Exceat Hill before passing close to the Park Centre at Exceat Farm.

The Golden Galleon

The Golden Galleon, built in 1934 on the site of a much smaller building, is a rambling pub which is able to cope effortlessly with a large volume of business, particularly during the summer months. The extensive interior is a honeycomb of dining and drinking areas, decorated in the arts and crafts style of the period and incorporating old ship's timbers which, no doubt, inspired the name of the pub. The bar opens out onto a large garden on a bank overlooking the Cuckmere River. The pub prides itself on its large selection of real ales, with up to twelve beers and seven ciders on the go at one time, including Cuckmere Haven Best Bitter and Golden Peace, brewed on the premises. The food menu is a large one, with a strong Italian emphasis and vegetarians are well catered for. Bar snacks include salads and a range of ploughman's.

Opening times are from 10 am (for morning coffee – alcohol from 11 am) to 11 pm on Monday to Saturday, 12 noon to 10.30 pm on Sunday (closed Sunday evening in winter). Food is served from 12 noon to 2.30 pm and 6 pm to 9 pm (all day on summer weekends). Telephone: 01323 892247.

The Walk

① From the pub cross Exceat Bridge over the Cuckmere River and, after 60 yards, turn right through a swing gate and follow a clear path on a raised bank beside a canalised section of the river. As the path approaches the mouth of the Cuckmere it

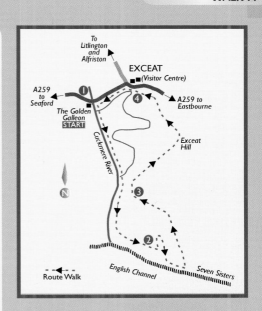

veers left, heading for the cliffs rising steeply on the eastern side of the haven and continuing along the foot of a grassy bank, rising up to your left.

② Cross the main track to the beach and continue to a T-junction at the foot of the steep slope. Turn left here, following a waymarked path diversion which, after about 150 yards, goes right through a gate and then doubles back to the right on a path which heads for the sea, climbing steadily across an area of downland pasture, close cropped by sheep and some specially imported Shetland ponies. As it approaches the cliff edge, the path veers left up to the top of the

PLACES OF INTEREST NEARBY

While in the area, spare time to visit the village of **Alfriston**, about 4 miles up the valley. Next to the church and village green is the thatched 14th century **Clergy House**, a National Trust property.

Cuckmere Haven

first of the Seven Sisters where a sudden view opens out eastwards along the remainder of the Sisters and, beyond Birling Gap, to the disused lighthouse of Belle Tout, which was recently raised bodily from its foundations and moved inland when collapse into the sea seemed imminent. At the highest point, turn sharply back to the left past a three-armed finger post where your route is indicated as the South Downs Way to Exceat. Follow a path gently downhill with a fence on your left.

③ Back at valley level, go forward on a hard chalk and flint track for 150 yards. It joins a concrete access track where, if you have had enough of climbing, you can bear left along the valley to point 4. However,

for a much superior route go ahead through a swing gate with the South Downs Way which follows a grassy path up onto Exceat Hill. Go straight over a crossing path and gradually veer left across the shoulder of the hill. To the right of the highest point is a stone marker on the site of Exceat church, an 11th century building which fell into disuse and ruin following the ravages of the Black Death and frequent French raids. The path continues down to join the A259 opposite Exceat Farm, now a visitor centre, restaurant, tearooms and cycle hire shop.

④ Turn left and follow the raised path beside this busy road for ¹/₄ mile back to the Golden Galleon.

Arlington
The Old Oak Inn

MAP: OS EXPLORER 123 (GR 558077) | **WALK 15** | **DISTANCE:** 3 MILES

DIRECTIONS TO START: FROM WILMINGTON CROSSROADS ON THE A27 LEWES TO EASTBOURNE ROAD HEAD NORTH, SIGNPOSTED TO ARLINGTON. AT A T-JUNCTION TURN RIGHT, SIGNPOSTED TO UPPER DICKER. THE PUB IS ON THE LEFT AFTER ½ MILE.
PARKING: IN THE PUB CAR PARK, BUT, IDEALLY, LET THE LANDLORD KNOW.

This is a nicely contrasted walk. It starts out along field paths in the valley of the Cuckmere River, soon passing Michelham Priory (see Places of Interest). It then winds through Bramble Grove, a fine spot for bluebells in the spring, before returning across the sandy heath of Milton Hide. The walk can easily be extended into the Forestry Enterprise area of Abbot's Wood, using one of several paths to the left beyond point 4. This option has the advantage of avoiding a muddy and overgrown stretch of bridleway but you will need a map and, ideally, a compass to find your way back to the start. Alternatively, as an add-on to the walk, drive to the official Forestry car park, just down the road from the pub at GR 558072 and follow one of the well waymarked trails. The 'Abbot's Amble', about a mile in length and marked with yellow footprint signs, takes in the old abbey fish ponds.

The Old Oak Inn

The premises now occupied by the Old Oak started life in the early 18th century as a row of four almshouses. One hundred years later, one of the cottages was converted into an alehouse for the local charcoal burners from Abbot's Wood and the full pub conversion followed in due course. Today you and your dog will be welcomed by Henrietta, the basset hound, into the spacious bar area with its low oak beams hung with dried hops and a large open fireplace at one end. Adjoining is a pleasant dining area and, outside, a sheltered garden. The Old Oak is a free house and the real ales come straight from the cask - Harveys Sussex and Badger Best at all times plus a guest beer. The lunchtime menu has a wide enough choice for the hungriest walker, including a home made soup of the day and a range of snacks including filled baguettes and jacket potatoes. More substantial dishes on offer include steak and Guinness pie and a vegetarian choice.

Opening hours are Monday to Saturday from 11am to 3pm and 6pm to 11pm, Sunday from 12noon to 3pm and 7pm to 10.30pm. Food is served daily from 12noon to 2pm and 7pm to 9pm. Children are welcome. Telephone: 01323 482072.

The Walk

① From the pub turn left (north) along the lane. Shortly, go left through the entrance to Primrose Farm and, after 10 yards, bear right along a concrete farm track. After about 200 yards, where the

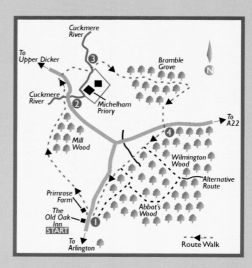

concrete surface ends, turn right through a gate and head diagonally out across a field. In the far field corner, go through a gate and maintain your previous direction across the next field, passing squarely under power lines about 30 yards to the left of a pylon. Go through a gate and forward across the corner of a meadow. You have a choice of two gates ahead. Go through the one on the right and on along a right field edge with a wood on your right. Follow this good headland track out to join a road over a stile a few yards to the left of a gate.

② Turn left, cross the Cuckmere River

PLACES OF INTEREST NEARBY

The moated Augustinian **Michelham Priory**, passed on the walk, incorporates the remains of the abbey buildings plus a Tudor mansion and a striking 14th century gatehouse. It is owned by the Sussex Archaeological Society and is open from mid-March to late October from Wednesday to Sunday (every day in August). For detailed opening times, telephone 01323 844224.

Michelham Priory

and, on your right, the entrance to Michelham Priory. After another 150 yards or so, turn right over a stile and bear half-right, following a right field edge. In the field corner go through a gate and over a stile, now on the well-signed Wealdway which heads diagonally across a field before passing to the left of a barn.

③ Turn left across a bridge over the Cuckmere which, at this point, is the outlet stream from the moat surrounding Michelham Priory. Go forward along a track to cross another bridge and bear right through a long thin field, walking parallel to the hedge on your left. At the far end of the field go through a gateway. At this point the Wealdway goes off to the left but you should go ahead across rough pasture to enter a wood (Bramble Grove) over a stile. Go ahead on a defined woodland path, ignoring side paths. Leave the wood through a rudimentary gate and go forward along a right field edge with the wood now on your right. In the field corner follow the field edge round to your left and, in the next field corner, go right over a stile beside a gate. Turn right along a wide track, once very muddy but now well drained and laid with hard core. Follow it for a little over ¼ mile out to a road. Turn left.

④ Shortly, when you are standing beneath minor power lines, turn sharply back to the right between two low wooden posts and along a trodden path, beneath the power lines at first, then diverging to the left of them, across an area of patchy heath and scrub. Ignore side paths. After entering thicker woodland, cross a wide bridle bridge and continue along a narrower, overgrown path out to rejoin the road. Turn left back to the start.

Mark Cross
The Mark Cross Inn

MAP: OS EXPLORER 136 (GR 582312)	**WALK 16**	DISTANCE: 3 MILES

DIRECTIONS TO START: MARK CROSS IS AT THE JUNCTION OF THE A267 HEATHFIELD TO TUNBRIDGE WELLS ROAD AND THE B2100 ABOUT 7 MILES NORTH OF HEATHFIELD. THE PUB IS A FEW YARDS ALONG THE B2100 TO THE EAST OF THE ROAD JUNCTION. **PARKING:** YOU CAN PARK IN THE LARGE PUB CAR PARK WITH PERMISSION. THERE IS AN ALTERNATIVE FREE CAR PARK SQUEEZED BETWEEN THE A267 AND THE B2100 A FEW YARDS SOUTH OF THE PUB.

This is a delightful walk, deep in the High Weald. Starting high on a ridge at the head of the long valley carved by the Eastern River Rother and its many feeder streams, it takes an undulating route, crossing and recrossing a quiet wooded valley. Some of the footpaths in the area are little used and navigation requires care. At one point, at the time of writing, a minor diversion has been necessary to avoid a blocked path. This may change so watch for signs and have a map to hand in case you do go astray. Part of the walk passes through an area designated under the Countryside Stewardship Scheme. Public access within this area is assured at least until September 2002 when the agreement with the landowner may or may not be renewed. The right of way used on the walk will remain permanently open.

The Mark Cross Inn

Now set back from the main road but once on a busy crossroads, the Mark Cross Inn is a large and welcoming pub for walkers. The premises were developed and expanded some years ago by the linking together of two existing buildings, allowing extra space for a large open bar area and a separate restaurant. Even so, it can get very crowded at Sunday lunchtime. A sheltered patio at the rear offers one of the finest pub views in Sussex, south-eastwards down the whole length of the upper Rother valley. The tempting 'Terrace Menu', available at lunchtime, offers a wide selection of bar snacks including filled baguettes, open sandwiches, pasta dishes and jacket potatoes. More substantial main dishes and puddings are available as 'blackboard specials'. The pub is a Whitbread tied house but is free to choose its beers, currently the local Harveys Bitter and Fuller's London Pride plus a guest beer during the summer months. Opening times are 11 am to 3 pm and 6 pm to 11 pm on weekdays, 12 noon to 3 pm on Sundays (closed Sunday evenings). Telephone: 01892 852423.

The Walk

① From the entrance to the pub car park turn left, ignoring the left turn to Wadhurst, and walk back towards the A267/B2100 junction. Go through the second gate on your left and walk downhill with a hedge, left, to a culvert and climb with a hedge, right. Go over a stile and turn left within a copse, passing a

pond on your right. Leave the wood and turn right on a track which passes between the buildings at Renhurst Farm and drops downhill along a headland. Go through a gate and climb along a right field edge to join Lake Street. Turn left.

② Soon after passing the red brick and tile hung farmhouse at Little Trodgers on your left, turn left along the drive to Little Trodgers Oast. This becomes an unmade track and then a waymarked path, parallel and to the left of an equestrian circuit. Beyond another gate turn right, contouring along the upper edge of three fields.

③ At the end of the third field the right of way officially doubles back to the left but is partially obstructed further on and unusable at present. Instead, just short of a gate turn left for 10 yards, side step

PLACES OF INTEREST NEARBY

About a mile to the north of Mark Cross, to the east of the A267 is **Nap Wood**, 45 acres of ancient oak woodland, managed as a nature reserve with a laid-out trail for visitors.

The view back to Mark Cross from Renhurst Farm

through a gap on your right and resume your previous direction, downhill with a hedge, left. At the bottom go left through another gap and follow a right field edge with a wood on your right until you can enter the wood, cross a wide bridge and climb up through the wood on a clear well trodden path.

④ Where the path divides, fork right up to a stile and follow a faint path half-left across rough pasture. Drop down with a house and garden on your right. Cross a drive and a soggy dip and climb along the right edge of a field. Beyond a stile a few yards to the left of the top field corner, continue along a woodland path.

⑤ At a junction with a wide track turn right following it round to the left, ignoring a track to the right and soon descending. Where the main track bears left, continuing downhill, turn sharply back to the right on a narrower path, up through a coppice and an area of woodland and on across a paddock to join a road. Turn left.

⑥ After about 150 yards turn right over a stile and head out across a field, aiming just to the right of a prominent converted windmill, to find a stile. Make your way out via a short enclosed path and the access drive from the mill to the A267. Turn left back to the start.

Vines Cross
The Brewer's Arms

MAP: OS EXPLORER 123 (GR 594178)	WALK 17	DISTANCE: 2¼ MILES

DIRECTIONS TO START: VINES CROSS IS SIGNPOSTED FROM THE B2096 HEATHFIELD TO BATTLE ROAD ABOUT A MILE EAST OF HEATHFIELD, FOLLOWING UNCLASSIFIED ROADS VIA OLD HEATHFIELD. ALTERNATIVELY, APPROACH FROM THE WEST, LEAVING THE A267 HEATHFIELD TO EASTBOURNE ROAD AT HORAM. **PARKING:** YOU ARE WELCOME TO USE THE BREWER'S ARMS CAR PARK WHILE ON THE WALK.

The southern slopes of the High Weald are formed by a series of gentle hills dropping down from the main sandstone ridge linking Heathfield with Battle. These low ridges are separated by valleys carved by streams draining into the Cuckmere River or Waller's Haven (see Walk 22). On this walk we cross and recross one such valley, climbing to the hilltop hamlet of Warbleton where the church with its solid sandstone tower is strikingly situated on the summit of the ridge. Inside is a fine 15th century brass and, in the churchyard, a memorial to Richard Woodman, a local ironmaster who was one of the Protestant martyrs, burned with nine others in Lewes in 1557. Across the lane from the church is a fine row of weathered red brick cottages, partly dating from 1739 and once the local workhouse.

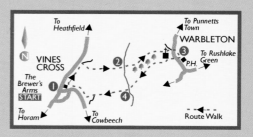

The Brewer's Arms

The Brewer's Arms has been a pub since 1753 when ale was served from what is now the Tap Room, the smallest of a series of cosy dining and drinking areas which open from each other to form the present premises. Although owned by Greene King, this is very much a traditional country pub, run in the same way by the same family for the last 40 years. The main bar, partly lined by bookshelves, is festooned with an idiosyncratic assortment of rural paraphernalia as well as two vintage bicycles and a penny-farthing. The pub has a garden and well-equipped children's play area. The extensive and varied food menu offers what must be among the best value pub grub in the county. If you have the constitution for it, try one of the impressive gut-busting grills, the home made bacon pudding or the exceptional ham, egg and chips, always a good test dish by which to judge the food in a pub and one which the Brewer's Arms passes with flying colours. The beer, available in cut price four-pint jugs as well as by the pint, is Greene King Abbot Ale, Morland Old Speckled Hen and Harveys Sussex Bitter.

Opening hours are 11 am to 3 pm and 6 pm to 11 pm on Monday to Saturday, 12 noon to 3 pm and 7 pm to 10.30 pm on Sunday. Food is available daily except Monday lunchtime. Children and dogs are welcome. Telephone: 01435 812288.

The Walk

① From the pub turn right along the lane, back in the Heathfield direction. After about 350 yards, about 60 yards past the aptly named Wisteria Cottages on your left, turn right along the drive to Boring House Farm. Immediately past a cattle grid, leave the drive by forking right across a grassy dip and up to a stile, in sight, providing access into a copse. Follow a path within the left edge of this wood and then go forward along the left edge of two fields, dropping gently down into a wide valley.

② Cross a footbridge over an iron-coloured stream and head gently up across the next field, passing squarely under power lines. In the top left field corner go over a stile and continue very gently uphill with a wood on your right and a good view across the valley to your left towards Heathfield, with the church spire at Old Heathfield in clear view. In the field corner go over a stile and continue with a wood on your right at

PLACES OF INTEREST NEARBY

The **Cuckoo Trail**, on the track bed of an old railway, passes about a mile to the west of Vines Cross, and offers 11 miles of easy level walking between Polegate and Heathfield, punctuated by specially commissioned sculptures beside the path. It is also part of the National Cycle Network.

Warbleton, visited on the walk

first. Where the field boundary on your right turns sharply back to the right, go ahead along an unfenced path. Just short of Warbleton churchyard, turn left and follow a post and rail fence round and out to a lane. Turn right.

③ After less than 60 yards, with the War Bill in Tun pub in sight ahead, turn right through the main entrance to Warbleton church. Skirt to the left of the church and, when opposite the church tower on your right, turn left through a gap in a wall (to your right is the memorial to Richard Woodman – see introduction). Cross a corner of the churchyard to a stile and go ahead, dropping down across a field. On the other side of the field turn left at the foot of a low bracken-covered bank. After a little over 200 yards, side step to the right through a gap in the hedge on your right and resume your previous direction with this hedge now on your left. About 50 yards short of the bottom field corner veer half-right, passing under power lines.

④ Go over a substantial footbridge, veer slightly right across a field to a gate and continue in the same direction up across a second field. In the top right field corner go through a gateway and forward along a left field edge out to a lane. Turn right back into Vines Cross.

Punnetts Town
The Three Cups Inn

MAP: OS EXPLORER 124 (GR 635201)	**WALK 18**	**DISTANCE:** 2 MILES

DIRECTIONS TO START: PUNNETTS TOWN IS ON THE B2096 HEATHFIELD TO BATTLE ROAD ABOUT 3 MILES EAST OF HEATHFIELD. THE PUB IS AT THREE CUPS CORNER ABOUT A MILE TO THE EAST OF THE MAIN VILLAGE. **PARKING:** THE PUB HAS A LARGE CAR PARK WHICH PUB PATRONS ARE WELCOME TO USE WHILE ON THE WALK.

Punnetts Town stands high on one of the so-called forest ridges which extend eastwards from Heathfield towards Battle and Hastings. Straddling both sides of the ridge, our walk offers a succession of sweeping views, first to the north across the lovely wooded valley of the River Dudwell, then southwards to the distant ridge of the South Downs between Eastbourne and Lewes.

Punnetts Town Windmill, a fine smock mill, was removed from Biddenden in Kent and rebuilt here in 1856 to replace an older post mill. By 1947 it had fallen into ruin but has been painstakingly restored to its former glory, including machinery, fan tail and sails. It is not open to the public but the walk passes close by. After dropping down the south slope of the ridge, a steady climb up though the delightful Kemp's Wood provides a fine climax to the walk.

The Three Cups Inn

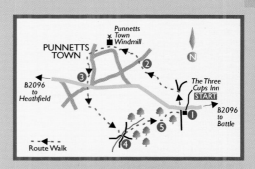

Standing back from the road and surrounded by spacious grounds, this welcoming family pub is perfectly situated amidst some of the best walking country in Sussex. The spacious bar has a large open fire and, at the rear, a family room opens out to a covered terrace and a sheltered garden. The Three Cups Inn was developed from two cottages and a pre-existing alehouse and is a tied pub, originally developed by the now defunct Star Brewery at Eastbourne and currently owned by Greene King, the 200 year old Suffolk brewery. The inn sign depicts three stirrup cups but the name of the pub and the corner on which it stands may derive more obscurely from the fact that it occupies the watershed separating the sources of three streams.

Beers on offer include Harveys Sussex Ale, Greene King IPA and Wadworth 6X and there is a short list of reasonably priced wines. The food is all home cooked with several chef's specials such as fish pie or toad in the hole always available, together with a full range of standard pub dishes and bar snacks. The pub is open from 11.30 am to 3 pm and 6.30 pm to 11 pm Monday to Friday, 11 am to 11 pm on Saturday and 12 noon to 10.30 pm on Sunday. Food is served from 12 noon to 2.15 pm and 6.30 pm to 9.15 pm except Sunday evenings. Telephone: 01435 830252.

The Walk

① From the pub cross the B2096 to follow a drive, almost opposite, signed as a bridleway which soon becomes a hedged track. After about 200 yards, fork left and left again over a stile. Go forward along a left field edge until you can side step to the left over a stile and continue with a fence on your right. A path squeezes to the right of buildings, keeps to the right of the next field and, in the field beyond, veers half-left. Cross a stile and follow an enclosed path out to a lane.

② Follow the drive to Blackdown Farm, opposite. Shortly go left round two sides of a paddock to a stile and ahead across the corner of a grassy area to another stile to the left of a yellow painted post. An enclosed path continues out to a lane. Turn right passing Punnetts Town Windmill. At a road junction bear left and continue out to the B2096.

③ Turn right and immediately fork left

PLACES OF INTEREST NEARBY

A few miles to the east, in and around the village of **Brightling**, and worth seeking out, can be found a number of follies, including a tower, an obelisk and a fake church spire called the Sugar Loaf. They are all the work of John 'Mad Jack' Fuller, an 18th century eccentric who is buried beneath a pyramidal stone mausoleum in Brightling churchyard.

The Dudwell valley

along a lane. Almost immediately go left over a stile hidden behind a small electricity substation and ahead along a left field edge. In the field corner cross a stile and turn left along the drive to a cottage. Just short of the cottage bear left along the top of a grassy bank. Go through an iron gate behind the cottage and drop down gently along the right edge of two fields. Once into a third field, veer half-left down to a stile and footbridge in the bottom field corner leading into Kemp's Wood.

④ After a few yards, at a path junction turn sharply left up steps to a stile leading out into a field corner. Immediately, turn left over a second stile, re-entering the wood. After 30 yards, at a path junction, fork right and climb steadily. Leave the wood over another stile and continue with the wood on your left at first. Go forward over a stile and uphill with a hedge, left.

⑤ In the field corner go left through two gates and then slightly right across a paddock to a stile. A well-trodden path takes you through an area of scrubby woodland to a lane. Turn left back to the start, a few yards away.

Wadhurst
The Rock Robin Inn

MAP: OS EXPLORER 136
(GR 621330)

WALK 19

DISTANCE: 3 MILES

DIRECTIONS TO START: THE ROCK ROBIN INN IS ABOUT A MILE WEST OF WADHURST VILLAGE CENTRE, ON THE B2099 ROAD OPPOSITE WADHURST RAILWAY STATION. EASIEST ROAD ACCESS IS ALONG THE B2099 FROM THE A267 HEATHFIELD TO TUNBRIDGE WELLS ROAD SOUTH OF FRANT. **PARKING:** YOU MAY PARK IN THE PUB CAR PARK, BUT MAKE YOURSELF KNOWN TO THE PUB AS THE LANDLORD HAS PROBLEMS WITH UNAUTHORISED PARKING BY TRAIN COMMUTERS.

From the pub this varied walk heads north on an undulating route over low ridges and across tranquil well wooded valleys carved by branches of a tiny stream draining northwards into the River Teise, a tributary of the Medway. For some of the way you will be walking along deep-cut sunken tracks which burrow through patches of thick woodland, often between high sandstone banks and possibly muddy underfoot, particularly after rain. Several of the cottages passed on the walk are clad in the white weatherboarding which is such a charming and characteristic feature of the buildings in this part of the northern High Weald near the Sussex/Kent border. Part of the walk follows a section of the Sussex Border Path, a long distance walkers' route using paths on or near the county boundary for 150 miles between Emsworth and Rye.

The Rock Robin Inn

Housed in a fairly modern 1930s building, the Rock Robin is a friendly family run free house incorporating a spacious traditionally furnished bar and a small dining room. Outside there is a paved patio and a sheltered lawn at the rear, open at weekends during the summer months. The pub prides itself on its beer with six well-kept real ales on the go including, at all times, Harveys Sussex and Summer Lightning from the Hop Back Brewery in Salisbury as well as regularly changed guest beers such as Adnams Regatta. The extensive food menu is all prepared and cooked on the premises and includes most of the pub favourites as well as some less usual dishes such as Jamaican chicken curry and, notably, a range of speciality pizzas.

The pub is open Monday to Saturday from 11 am to 11 pm and Sundays from 12 noon to 10.30 pm. Food is served from 12 noon to 2 pm and 6.30 pm to 9 pm. Dogs on leads are welcome as are children in the restaurant area. Telephone: 01892 783776.

The Walk

① From the pub turn left along the B2099. Just short of the Four Keys pub, turn sharply back to the left along a concrete access. In front of a row of cottages, turn left along a narrow path. Walk straight through a garden, passing to the left of a house incorporating a striking octagonal brick and weatherboarded tower, and on along another narrow path. On reaching the end of an access drive to some

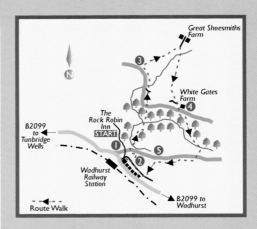

cottages, fork right uphill along another enclosed path which tunnels between banks and descends to join a lane.

② Turn left and, after a little over 100 yards, turn right along a fenced path, signed as a bridleway. Follow it for almost ¹/₂ mile, across two streams and passing through two areas of woodland to join a lane and turn left. Follow this lane across another valley.

③ After about ¹/₄ mile turn sharply back to the right along the metalled drive to Great Shoesmiths Farm. About 100 yards short of the farm buildings turn sharply back to the right over a brick bridge and along an unmade drive lined by a row of young lime trees. Join a concrete drive and bear right to follow it out to a lane at White Gates Farm.

PLACES OF INTEREST NEARBY

Bewl Water, a few miles to the east, covers 770 acres and is the largest stretch of inland water in south-east England. It has a visitor centre and offers cycles for hire and boat trips during the summer months.

Great Shoesmiths Farm

④ Turn left and, after 10 yards only, go right over a stile to the left of a drive. A clear path descends through a wood, bearing left in front of a gate. Where the track divides, fork right downhill to cross a ford. Just short of another gate, bear right on a fenced path up to a lane. Turn right.

⑤ After ¹/₄ mile you will come to three driveways, in quick succession, on your left. Yours is the one in the middle, marked as a footpath, which soon narrows briefly to a path. Cross a drive and the stile opposite and bear left uphill beside a fence. At the top, cross another drive and go over an unusual ladder stile topped by a gate in a fence. Go forward skirting to the left of two rows of cottages and turn right along a rough access track. Rejoin your outgoing route bearing left down to the B2099 by the Four Keys and right back to the pub.

Burwash Weald
The Wheel Inn

MAP: OS EXPLORER 124 (GR 651232)	**WALK 20**	DISTANCE: 3 OR 3½ MILES

DIRECTIONS TO START: BURWASH WEALD IS ON THE A265 HEATHFIELD TO HURST GREEN ROAD ABOUT 5 MILES EAST OF HEATHFIELD AND THE WHEEL INN IS ON THE NORTH SIDE OF THE ROAD. **PARKING:** YOU ARE WELCOME TO PARK IN THE PUB CAR PARK WHILE ON THE WALK IF ALSO PATRONISING THE PUB.

This walk explores a remote and peaceful valley carved by the River Dudwell, a modest feeder stream of the Eastern Rother. It follows a delightfully contrasting sequence of field and woodland paths on the northern slope of the valley as well as offering a gentle stroll through riverside meadows and along a shady path beside the Dudwell. This is the landscape which inspired Rudyard Kipling to write the children's stories *Puck of Pook's Hill* and *Rewards and Fairies* and a short there-and-back extension to the walk will allow you to visit his former home. Bateman's, a fine stone mansion, was built by a local ironmaster in 1634 and occupied by Kipling between 1902 and 1936. En route to the house the walk passes the mill pond and water mill used by Kipling to generate electricity.

The Wheel Inn

Unusually, the small community of Burwash Wheel was originally named after its first pub, an earlier hostelry called the 'Catherine Wheel' in honour of Henry VIII's first wife, Catherine of Aragon. Converted into a poorhouse when the present pub was built in 1760, Wheel became Weald to avoid inappropriate associations with a drinking establishment. In 1834 The Wheel was described by visitors from Portsmouth as 'one of the roughest public houses they had been in'. A notorious haunt for smugglers and criminals, it has been the scene of brawls with excise men and even a murder. This turbulent past is now long gone and the modern traveller enjoys a far more tranquil reception into the spacious bar area and adjacent dining and games rooms. Walkers, dogs and children are made equally welcome to this relaxed and friendly establishment. The Wheel is a free house, offering an extensive food menu including a good vegetarian selection and daily 'specials' such as lamb stew or marinated venison steak and a Sunday lunch carvery. The beers on hand pump always include Harveys Sussex Ale and Fuller's London Pride. Conveniently the pub is open daily from 12 noon to 11 pm and food is served right through the afternoon and up to 10 at night. Telephone: 01435 882758 or visit the comprehensively detailed pub web site at www.thewheel.co.uk

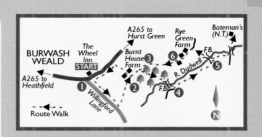

The Walk

① From the pub start the walk along Willingford Lane, opposite. About half way down the hill, just past a cottage on the left called Hedge Nest, go left through a swing gate and along a left field edge to a second swing gate. Now veer half-left. In the field corner go through a bridle gate and across a field aiming just to the right of the buildings of Burnt House Farm.

② Just short of the buildings go right over a stile. Cross a small paddock to a second stile and go forward with an iron fence on your left, past two massive oak trees.

③ Just short of a gate in the field corner veer half-right and drop downhill with a hedge, left, and down through Bog Wood, a delightful path. Towards the bottom of the hill, leave the wood and follow a right field edge until you can turn right over a wide bridge across the Dudwell.

PLACES OF INTEREST NEARBY

The house and garden at **Bateman's**, visited on the extended walk or accessible by road via Burwash, 2 miles to the east of Burwash Weald, is owned by the National Trust and is open from April to the end of October, daily except Thursday and Friday, from 11 am to 5 pm. It has a shop and tearoom.

Burnt House Farm

④ Turn left along the valley. Where you have a choice of gates go through the one on the right and forward along a field edge. After 150 yards go left over a wide farm bridge, then bear right along the length of a meadow, with the river away to your left. Path and river converge and, beyond a stile, meander on through a belt of woodland.

⑤ After about 150 yards, the direct return route goes left over a substantial bridge across the Dudwell. (For the extension to Bateman's go ahead here, past the mill pond to join a drive and turn left. Return the same way.) Once over the bridge at point 5 go ahead across a meadow to join and follow a hedge, right. In the field corner go right over a culvert and immediately left along a left field edge to a stile and on along a hedged track which passes two barns at Rye Green Farm.

⑥ Join the metalled access drive from a cottage and immediately fork left on a rough track which soon heads out, unfenced, across a large field, climbing gently. Go forward through a belt of trees, up across a field to a gap in the top corner and on with a hedge, right. Back at point 3, reverse your steps past the two oak trees and across the paddock to point 2. Now turn right to a gate and go forward between the buildings at Burnt House Farm. Follow the farm access drive out to the A265 and turn left back to the start.

Brownbread Street
The Ash Tree Inn

MAP: OS EXPLORER 124 (GR 676149)

WALK 21

DISTANCE: 4½ MILES

DIRECTIONS TO START: FROM THE A271 HERSTMONCEUX TO BATTLE ROAD TURN LEFT AT GR 685135. TAKE THE FIRST TURNING TO THE LEFT AND KEEP RIGHT AT THE NEXT ROAD JUNCTION. THE PUB IS ON THE LEFT ABOUT A MILE FROM THE MAIN ROAD. **PARKING:** YOU MAY PARK IN THE PUB CAR PARK OR THE LAY-BY AREA OPPOSITE THE PUB.

The hamlet of Brownbread Street needs to be sought out, one of several tiny settlements which make up the parish of Ashburnham. The area was once at the centre of the Wealden iron industry but is now a quiet and remote landscape of gently rolling hills and peaceful valleys on the southern slopes of the High Weald. The walk explores a patchwork of fields and small areas of residual woodland and, between points 3 and 4, follows one of the ancient trackways, sometimes known as green lanes, which are such a characteristic feature of the area. Some of the paths are little used and not always obvious. Follow the directions with care, particularly near the start where the path from the road north of the pub is indistinct and overgrown in places. Although longer than most walks in this book, the last mile and a half offers easy going along quiet country lanes.

The Ash Tree Inn

Several hundred years old and constructed from warm red brick and local indigenous hung tiles, the Ash Tree offers a particularly warm welcome to walkers. It is a free house, owned by the Ashburnham Estate but independently managed. Opening from the main bar and a relatively modern games room at one end, the older part of the pub is divided into four snug low-beamed rooms on two levels, three with open fires in winter. There is a hedged garden at the rear. Children and dogs are welcome. The regularly changed blackboard menu offers a number of specialities. Choose from roast half shoulder of local organically reared lamb, a large seafood platter for two, a range of steaks and chops, steak and ale pie or vegetarian options, mostly home made. The snack menu includes a range of ploughman's, jacket potatoes and filled baps or baguettes. The beers on hand pump are Harveys Sussex and Morland Old Speckled Hen plus a rotating guest beer at times of peak demand.

The opening hours are 12 noon to 3 pm and 7 pm to 11 pm Monday to Saturday, 12 noon to 3 pm and 7 pm to 10.30 pm on Sundays. Telephone: 01424 892104.

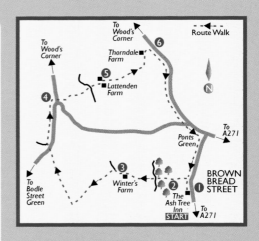

The Walk

① From the pub turn left along the lane. After about 150 yards go left over a stile and forward for a few yards through an overgrown area of grass and thin scrub to another stile. Drop down with a hedge, right. Cross a gully and turn left with this gully to your left. Cross another shallow dip and bear half-left up across rough grass to a stile.

② Follow the direction of an arrow on the stile squarely across a large field. On the other side a faint path winds down through woodland to a footbridge and up to a stile. Head out across a field, go through a gate in the far right corner and on along a field edge and through two more gates. On reaching a cottage on your left bear right along the cottage access drive.

③ Shortly go left through two gates in quick succession and follow a hedged path downhill, over a footbridge, up through woodland and on along the right edge of

PLACES OF INTEREST NEARBY

While in the area, spare time to visit **Penhurst** about a mile to the north. Once a bustling centre of the iron smelting industry, it is now a tiny secluded hamlet, comprising little more than a charming 14th century church with a 'Sussex cap' tower and, next door, a 17th century farmhouse.

Patchwork fields and woodland are a feature of this walk

two fields. In the second field corner go right through a gate. Follow a hedged track for ¹/₂ mile out to a lane and bear right.

④ After ¹/₄ mile, keep left, signposted to Wood's Corner. After 30 yards go right along a dirt track. Ignore the first gate on your right. After a few more yards go through another gate and along a right field edge to a third gate. Now descend to a stile in the bottom left field corner. Cross a footbridge in a wooded dip and follow power lines up across a field to a gate.

⑤ Follow a concrete drive between farm buildings, soon bearing left for a few yards to find a stile to the right of a gate. Climb steeply up a grassy slope with a fence, left. At the top go left over a stile and across a field to a stile in the far right corner, not in sight at first. Head out across the next field walking parallel to a hedge away to your right. Pass to the right of a derelict pond surrounded by trees, and immediately go left over a hidden stile. Walk half-right across a field to a gate to the right of barns at Thorndale Farm and right along the farm access drive to join a lane.

⑥ Turn right. At a road junction at the tiny hamlet of Ponts Green, go ahead. Just past the gateway to a house called Freedland Oast, fork right on a short path through to another lane. Turn right for a little over ¹/₂ mile back to the start.

Normans Bay
The Star Inn

MAP: OS EXPLORER 124 (GR 686060)	WALK 22	DISTANCE: 2½ MILES

DIRECTIONS TO START: FROM THE ROUNDABOUT AT THE EASTERN END OF THE PEVENSEY BYPASS ON THE A27/A259 EASTBOURNE TO HASTINGS ROAD, FOLLOW AN UNCLASSIFIED ROAD SIGNPOSTED TO NORMANS BAY. THE PUB IS 2½ MILES ALONG THIS NARROW LANE.
PARKING: YOU MAY PARK IN THE PUB CAR PARK WHILE ON THE WALK.

The drained marshland of Pevensey Levels was once an inland sea dotted with islands, identified today by the Old English suffix 'eye'. The first attempts at land reclamation came in the form of a sea wall, built in 1282, but it was not until the course of the River Ashburn (now Waller's Haven) was permanently diverted that the sea was reliably excluded. This walk passes the site of the 'lost' village of Northeye, abandoned after frequent flooding in the late Middle Ages, and also follows the line of the old sea wall to the north of the Crooked Ditch. The area later became a centre for salt-making and is now a patchwork of lush meadows and arable fields criss-crossed by drainage ditches. Although sometimes rough underfoot and wet in places it is a fine walk with long views to the Downs, vast open skies and only the sheep and skylarks for company.

The Star Inn

Although only established as an inn, the 'Star of Bethlehem', during the 17th century, the building dates back to 1402 and was originally the Sluice House, occupied by the men who regulated the flow of the diverted river which still flows through the pub garden. In the 18th century the Star was a centre for smuggling, being close to a landing point for cargoes of French brandy, and was the site of frequent pitched battles between smugglers and excise men. It is now a busy holidaymakers' pub with a bar on two levels, spacious restaurant, games room and large garden. Efficiently dispensed from behind a servery, the large menu is noted for locally caught fish and also offers home made pies and a speciality 'sausage of the week' as well as a dedicated children's menu. Bar snacks in the form of baguettes and sandwiches are available on weekdays only from 12 noon to 6 pm. Beer drinkers are well served by a choice of seven real ales including Flowers and Adnams Bitter, Young's Special and Bombardier Premium Bitter from Charles Wells of Bedford, the largest family owned brewery in England. The Star is open all day, at least during the summer months. Telephone: 01323 762648.

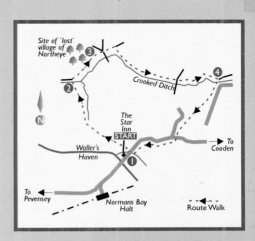

The Walk

① From the pub, turn left, cross a brick bridge over Waller's Haven and immediately turn left along a track beside the pub garden. Where this track ends at a gate, go forward over two stiles in quick succession and on in the same direction across pasture. The next stile, to the left of a gate, comes into sight as you cross a low summit with a fine view to your left of a wide sweep of the Downs between Firle Beacon and the hills above Eastbourne. Once over the stile, bear right, walking parallel to the fence on your right. At a marker post veer slightly left.

② Go over a stile and culvert which only comes into sight as you approach it and veer half-right across the next field, walking parallel with and about 50 yards away from a drainage channel on your right. The 'lost' village of Northeye, now marked only by a few bumps in the ground, once occupied the slightly raised area to your left.

PLACES OF INTEREST NEARBY

Pevensey, 2 miles to the west along the coast, is noted for its castle. First built by the Romans as the fortress of Anderida and patched up to fend off the Spanish Armada, it is now a picturesque ruin.

Crooked Ditch

③ Join a track and turn right across a wide sleeper bridge at a point where five footpaths meet, another indication that this was once a busy settlement. Go forward on a track between widely spaced hedges. After about 150 yards turn right over a collapsed stile in the hedge on your right and go forward for 30 yards to reach a drainage channel. Bear left and keep this reed-filled ditch on your right. Go over a stile about 30 yards to the left of the field corner and, shortly, ignore a footpath over a footbridge to your right. Go over a fixed gate, on through a soggy gap into the next field and forward along a meandering right field edge, still with a ditch (Crooked Ditch) on your right.

④ On reaching power lines, turn right, ignoring a culvert ahead. After a few yards, ignore another footbridge on your left. Instead, go forward over two stiles and on along the pleasant grassy right bank of a wide drainage channel. Cross a footbridge over a side channel and veer half-right across rough pasture which may be wet underfoot in places. Join a hedge, right, and follow it, now on a more substantial track, out to a lane. Turn right back to the start.

Catsfield
The White Hart

MAP: OS EXPLORER 124 (GR 722137)	WALK 23	DISTANCE: 4 MILES

DIRECTIONS TO START: FROM THE A269 AT NINFIELD, ABOUT 4 MILES NORTH OF BEXHILL, FOLLOW THE B2204 BATTLE ROAD FOR 2 MILES TO CATSFIELD. THE PUB IS BESIDE THE MAIN ROAD.
PARKING: YOU MAY PARK IN THE SMALL CAR PARK, DUE FOR EXPANSION AT THE REAR. ALTERNATIVELY THE VILLAGE CAR PARK IS A FEW YARDS ALONG CHURCH LANE, OPPOSITE THE PUB.

This is a particularly varied walk on the gently undulating southern slopes of the High Weald. Starting through old parkland it passes close to a large angling establishment where several newly constructed ponds are now beginning to blend attractively into the landscape. It then traverses Powdermill Wood, where, as the name suggests, the trees were once harvested to produce charcoal for the manufacture of gunpowder at a mill beside Farthing Pond, deep in this now quiet valley. From here the walk can be extended through a woodland nature reserve, mostly alder, a tree which thrives in the wet conditions of this marshy valley along with flower species such as the golden saxifrage and the marsh marigold. The return route is along part of the 1066 Country Walk, a long-distance route linking Eastbourne and Rye, passing through a chestnut coppice and a plantation of Christmas trees.

The White Hart

The White Hart has been a pub since 1703 and, although recently refurbished, has not lost the friendly welcoming atmosphere of a village local. It comprises a single long bar and an adjacent dining area which also retains a pub ambience in the form of exposed timber beams and a large open fireplace. Dried hops hang from the beams and on the wall is a varnished wooden notice 'Hop Pickers Wanted. Hard Workers Only.' The landlord is at pains to point out that, in spite of an emphasis on good home made food, the White Hart remains very much a pub with none of the tables bookable in advance. The menu includes a range of traditional dishes such as half shoulder of Sussex lamb but runs to less usual offerings like spiced leek and smoky bacon bake. A full range of bar snacks and substantial puddings such as treacle sponge and home made apple pie complete a wide choice of fare. Sensibly, to ensure that they are always in optimum condition, only two beers are available on hand pump, currently Harveys Sussex Bitter and Bass on draught.

The White Hart is open from 11 am to 3 pm and 6 pm to 11 pm Monday to Saturday, 12 noon to 3 pm and 6 pm to 10.30 pm on Sunday, with food served throughout opening hours. Dogs are welcome, as are children in the dining area and the shady pub garden. Telephone: 01424 892650.

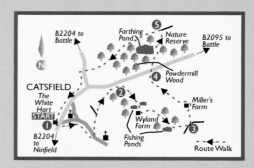

The Walk

① From the pub cross the B2204 road and follow Church Road, opposite. About 60 yards past the village school on the right, turn left through a gate and follow a fence uphill. Veer slightly left across the next field. Cross an iron ladder stile and go slightly right across parkland, aiming for a waypost at the corner of a wood. Cross a meadow, skirting to the right of a bungalow, to join the B2095. Turn right.

② After a little over 100 yards, turn right along the drive to an Angling Centre. At the Centre buildings, turn left along another drive. Where the drive divides, keep right. After another 100 yards, go ahead along a left field edge and on through woodland. Cross a footbridge, leave the wood over a stile and turn left along a field edge.

③ In the field corner go through a gate and turn left uphill along a fenced track. As you approach farm buildings at Miller's

PLACES OF INTEREST NEARBY

A visit to **Battle Abbey**, 3 miles away, includes the opportunity for a walk round the site of the Battle of Hastings, with explanatory panels. It is open throughout the year though times vary. Telephone: 01424 773792.

Catsfield

Farm, fork right over two stiles in quick succession and skirt round to the right of the farm area, keeping close to the perimeter fence, to join and bear right along the concrete access drive out to the B2095.

④ Go through a gate, almost opposite, and ahead on a broad track through Powdermill Wood, ignoring side paths. At the bottom go ahead over the outflow stream from Farthing Pond and across the earth dam beside the pond. On the other side of the dam, fork right and, after 10 yards, keep left on a path which climbs up through the wood. Leave the wood over a stile and cross a field to a second stile.

⑤ Turn left along a hedged track. After 650 yards, fork left over a stile by a gate and, ignoring a path to the left, climb steadily up through a coppice. At the top of the hill, turn right along a wide grassy path. Where the main track veers left, go ahead on a narrow path through a holly thicket. Leave the wood over a stile and follow a trodden path through a plantation of young conifers. Continue along a right field edge to a stile by a gate and along a track to the B2204. Turn left and after 60 yards go right over a stile and cross a field to rejoin the B2204. Turn right back to the start.

Hurst Green
The White Horse Inn

| **MAP:** OS EXPLORER 136 (GR 737260) | **WALK 24** | **DISTANCE:** 3 MILES |

DIRECTIONS TO START: HURST GREEN IS AT THE JUNCTION OF THE A21 HASTINGS TO MAIDSTONE ROAD WITH THE A265 FROM HEATHFIELD. THE WHITE HORSE IS BESIDE THE A21 AT SILVER HILL ABOUT $^3/_4$ MILE SOUTH OF THE VILLAGE. **PARKING:** PATRONS ARE WELCOME TO PARK IN THE PUB CAR PARK WHILE ON THE WALK.

This walk explores the northern slopes of the Rother valley to the south of Hurst Green. It starts with an easy climb up to the 360 foot summit of Silver Hill, a fine viewpoint. After a partial descent, a headland path contours along the lower valley slope, high enough to command a wide view along the river towards Etchingham and across the valley to the rolling well-wooded countryside to the east. The return route uses an old hollow way and then the main drive from Ockham House, lined on one side by a row of young lime trees and occasional Victorian-style lamp posts and on the other by a variety of mature specimens, notably hornbeam. Some of the paths in this remote area of the High Weald show little signs of use, particularly through the neglected meadow beyond point 4, so don't be discouraged if there is no well-trodden path.

The White Horse Inn

Although housed in a Grade II listed building, once a farmhouse, the White Horse Inn gives the impression of a modern spacious pub. From the large open plan bar and dining area you can walk out through French windows onto to a paved terrace and a large lawn with a superb view westwards across the Rother valley. The pub is a free house, family owned and run. The competitively priced home cooked menu includes old favourites like shepherd's pie and steak and kidney pie, all the usual bar snacks, a choice of vegetarian specialities and some solid puddings for hungry walkers such as spotted dick and jam roly poly. The landlord has sensibly set a limit of two well-kept ales on hand pump. Harveys Sussex and Charles Wells Bombardier are always available and a guest beer is added at weekends. Children are welcome in the pub but dogs are restricted to the garden. Opening hours are 12 noon to 3 pm and 6 pm to 11 pm from Monday to Saturday, 12 noon to 10.30 pm on Sunday. Telephone: 01580 860235.

The Walk

① From the pub cross the main road, turn right and immediately fork left, signposted to Staple Cross and Bodiam. After a few yards only, turn left along a metalled drive. After 350 yards, where the drive bends left, turn right along a grassy strip, soon bearing left and heading out across a field to join a wood edge. Climb with this wood on your left continuing up to the top of Silver Hill. Towards the top, look out for a half-hidden stile on the left.

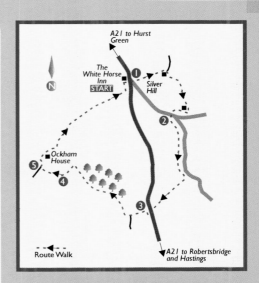

A narrow path skirts round two sides of a covered reservoir on your left and then right out to a lane. Turn right.

② After about 150 yards, turn sharply left along a narrow lane which soon drops down between high banks. Opposite a large house on the left, turn right through a gate and drop down along the left edge of two fields. Go over a drive, using two gates, and cross a meadow to join the A21 over a stile. Turn right.

③ After a few yards go left along a metalled drive which climbs between

PLACES OF INTEREST NEARBY

About 3 miles to the east is **Bodiam Castle**, built in 1385. Although now in ruins the grand exterior is virtually undamaged and, viewed across the surrounding moat, it presents a perfect embodiment of most people's idea of a romantic medieval castle. It is now in the hands of the National Trust and is open daily throughout the year. Telephone: 01580 830436.

The path near Silver Hill

banks. Where the drive bears left, go ahead over a stile and follow the right edge of three fields, contouring along the side of the valley at first. In the bottom corner of the third field go right through a gap in the hedge and left over a stile. Go forward for a few yards and then bear left, across a field, walking parallel to the hedge on your left.

④ Just short of a gap into the next field turn right, within the same meadow. Now follow the left edge of this and the next field. There is no path and, if the grass is long, the 'going' may be a bit heavy. Cross a track and go forward for a few yards across rough ground to join a sunken path.

⑤ Turn right and follow this path uphill. About 40 yards beyond a stile go left up some makeshift steps and right through a grassy area planted with young trees which narrows to a path and soon joins the drive from Ockham House. Go ahead along this drive for $1/2$ mile. About 100 yards short of the A21 fork left along a short length of redundant drive to join the main road over a stile. Turn left back to the start.

John's Cross
The John's Cross Inn

MAP: OS EXPLORER 124
(GR 743213)

WALK 25

DISTANCE: $3\frac{1}{2}$ MILES

DIRECTIONS TO START: JOHN'S CROSS AND THE PUB ARE ON THE A21 HASTINGS TO MAIDSTONE ROAD ABOUT 3 MILES SOUTH OF ROBERTSBRIDGE. THERE IS CONVENIENT ACCESS ALSO FROM BATTLE, NORTHWARDS ALONG THE A2100. **PARKING:** YOU ARE WELCOME TO USE THE PUB CAR PARK BUT PLEASE SEEK PERMISSION.

The tiny settlement of John's Cross, so called because it was once a marshalling point for Crusaders, stands high on a ridge separating two valleys carved by streams feeding northwards into the Eastern Rother. The walk straddles this ridge, starting past the impressive 18th century mansion of Mountfield Court. It then drops down into the wide valley of the Glottenham Stream, a lovely descent with superb views across to the wooded slopes on the other side of the valley as well as a glimpse of the Darwell Reservoir. A stroll along the valley follows, past former hop fields, now falling into dereliction. The return route climbs back over the ridge, returning to the pub across high ground to the north.

The John's Cross Inn

This lovely old pub dates back to 1511 and has been serving beer, on and off, at least since the end of the 17th century. Festooned in an eye-catching riot of flowers during the summer months, it makes a striking first impression. This is confirmed by the bright inn sign and various *trompe l'oeil* panels dotted round the premises, all the work of the landlord, Bob Russell, who operates a flourishing traditional sign-painting business from a studio at the rear of the pub. The cosy lounge bar, complete with a log fire in winter, has a tiny four-seater dining alcove at one end and there is a separate games room and public bar. The large sloping garden has one of the best pub views in the county. The traditional home cooked menu, supplemented by 'specials' such as steak and stilton pie or trout stuffed with asparagus and prawn sauce, offers enough variety to satisfy the choosiest walker. The real ales are from Greene King (IPA and Abbot) plus a regularly changed guest beer. Children are welcome, as are dogs, the latter in the public bar only.

Opening hours are 11.30 am to 3 pm and 6 pm to 11 pm Monday to Thursday, 11.30 am to 11 pm Friday and Saturday and 12 noon to 10.30 pm on Sunday. Food is served daily from 12 noon to 2.30 pm and 6.30 pm to 9 pm. Telephone: 01580 882154.

The Walk

① Start the walk along the 'No Through Road' opposite the pub, which beyond a

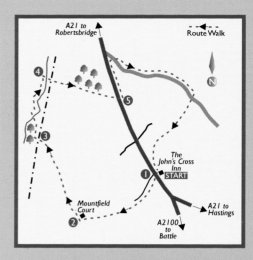

gateway becomes a private drive, lined by giant lime trees, though it remains a public footpath.

② Just after passing Mountfield Court on your right, turn right leaving the outbuildings to the mansion on your right and go ahead along an unmade track which begins to drop gently down into the valley. Where the track divides into three, go ahead through two gates and veer very slightly right, dropping downhill and passing a pond surrounded by trees. Go through a gate and continue downhill on a faint track.

③ At the bottom of the hill go under the railway and turn right beside the railway

PLACES OF INTEREST NEARBY

The large village of **Robertsbridge**, famed as a centre for the manufacture of cricket bats, lies 3 miles to the north and is well worth a visit. The High Street, now relieved of A21 traffic by a newish bypass, is lined by fine houses, some 600 years old.

The 18th century Mountfield Court

fence to a stile. A path winds through an area of patchy woodland to a footbridge. Cross a meadow to a second footbridge over the main Glottenham Stream. Immediately turn right along the right-hand edge of hop fields which may soon be no more as they appear untended and neglected.

④ After about 400 yards, go right over a stile and footbridge and immediately turn right across the railway. Head out across a low-lying meadow to a gate and go forward, following a hedge on your left. Cross a culvert and bear left, soon climbing along a field edge with a wood on your left. Go through a hedge gap beside a massive oak tree and directly ahead across a field to the A21.

⑤ Turn left beside the road. After 300 yards turn right along Poppinghole Lane and follow it for $^2/_3$ mile, down into a valley and up again. As the road levels out, turn right through a gate and go ahead, converging on the hedge to your left. In the field corner go through a gate in this hedge and maintain your previous direction, diverging slightly from the hedge on your right (if ploughed out follow the right field edge round). Go through a gate to the left of a pond and climb gently, walking parallel to a wood down the hill on your left. Go over a stile near the top left field corner and veer half-left across two more fields to join the A21 over a stile within yards of the pub.

Broad Oak, Brede
The Rainbow Trout

MAP: OS EXPLORER 124 OR 125 (GR 824198)	WALK 26	DISTANCE: 3½ MILES

DIRECTIONS TO START: BROAD OAK, BREDE NOT TO BE CONFUSED WITH ANOTHER BROAD OAK, NEAR HEATHFIELD, IS ON THE A28 HASTINGS TO TENTERDEN ROAD AT ITS JUNCTION WITH THE B2089 ABOUT 8 MILES NORTH OF HASTINGS. THE PUB IS BESIDE THE B2089 A FEW YARDS WEST OF THE ROAD JUNCTION.
PARKING: IN THE LARGE PUB CAR PARK, BUT PLEASE GET PERMISSION FIRST.

The parish of Brede is made up of three small settlements strung out along the A28 on the northern slopes of the valley of the River Brede, a tributary of the Rother – Broad Oak, Cackle Street and Brede itself. Starting high on the top of a ridge, this walk, while keeping clear of the main road, visits all three of these communities, dropping down almost to river level on good field paths which offer a series of unfolding views ahead across the Brede valley. The return route climbs gently, passing the church at Brede, with its sturdy 15th century tower, built mainly from sandstone and magnificently situated overlooking the valley. Brede also has a second pub, a simple village local, closed all day Monday and Tuesday lunchtime.

The Rainbow Trout

Originally two 18th century cottages, the Rainbow Trout occupies a superb position with a fine view southwards towards the Brede valley. The centrally placed spacious bar area leads into a non-smoking dining area at one end and a small comfortable conservatory at the rear. There is a large garden and children and dogs are welcomed. The pub is leased from Whitbreads but with freedom to choose from a wide selection of beers, currently Flowers Original and IPA plus Fuller's London Pride. Fish dishes, all home cooked, feature strongly on the extensive main menu, including Dover sole and grilled trout, locally caught. The pub also prides itself on its vegetarian choice such as mushroom and cashew nut tagliatelle or spinach and mushroom lasagne. Bar snacks are available except on Sunday lunchtime and include triple decker sandwiches, ploughman's and large crusty salad rolls with a choice of fillings, also a home-made soup of the day. To follow, try the Pancake Jubilee (black cherry and ice cream) or one of the speciality ice creams.

Opening hours are 11 am to 3 pm and 6 pm to 11 pm on Monday to Saturday, 12 noon to 3 pm and 7 pm to 10.30 pm on Sunday. Food is served daily from 12 noon to 2 pm and until 9.30 pm in the evening. Telephone: 01424 882436.

The Walk

① From the pub turn left along the B2089. Just past the last house on the

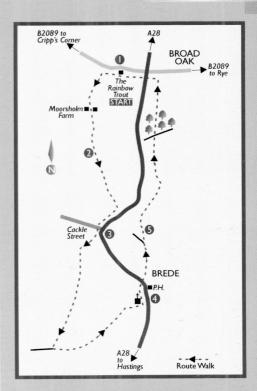

left, go left over a stile and along a left field edge. In the field corner go ahead along a fenced track and on between the buildings at Moorsholm Farm. Just beyond the farm buildings a sign directs you half-left along an unmade track.

② Where this track bears right and you have a choice of two gates, go ahead through the one on the left and keep to

PLACES OF INTEREST NEARBY

At Northiam, about 5 miles to the north along the A28, the famous garden of **Great Dixter**, home of the gardening guru Christopher Lloyd, is open during the summer months, as is the 15th century house with later additions by Sir Edward Lutyens. For details of opening times telephone 01797 252878.

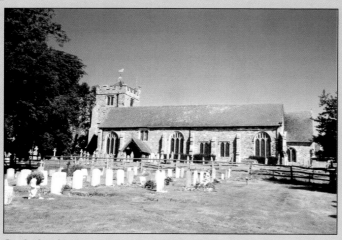

Brede church

past a turning to the right (Stubb Lane) and a bungalow called Willow Cottage, turn right along a narrow path. After a few yards join a grassy track and bear left, soon climbing along a right field edge. In the field corner cross a stile and keep to the right of the next field also. Soon after passing under power lines, where the trodden path divides, keep right (almost straight ahead) still along the right field edge.

the left of two fields, climbing gently at first. Walk out between buildings to join the A28 and turn right into Cackle Street.

③ At a junction with Pottery Lane go ahead over a stile between the two roads. Follow a trodden path half-right across a meadow and on between fences to a stile. Drop downhill, walking parallel to the meandering left edge of three fields with stiles between them and a fine view ahead across the Brede valley. At the bottom of the hill join a metalled drive and turn left to follow it uphill, finally passing Brede church to join the A28.

④ Turn left past the Red Lion pub. Just

⑤ Shortly, in the field corner, go over a stile and ahead across a field to the next stile, in sight. A hedged path continues, skirting to the right of several house gardens. Where the enclosed path ends, maintain direction across a field, walking parallel to power lines, a little to your right. On the far side of the field go over a crossing path, keeping to the left of a power pole to find a hidden stile. Follow a path through a wood to a gate. Go ahead along a left field edge to a stile, then on beside a fence, and out between buildings to join the B2089. Turn left. Cross the A28 and continue along the B2089, opposite, for the last few yards back to the pub.

Three Oaks
The Three Oaks

MAP: OS EXPLORER 124 (GR 839146)	**WALK 27**	DISTANCE: 2¾ MILES

DIRECTIONS TO START: THREE OAKS IS ABOUT 3 MILES NORTH OF HASTINGS AND CAN BE REACHED EITHER FROM THE A28 AT WESTFIELD TO THE WEST OR FROM THE A259 HASTINGS TO RYE ROAD TO THE EAST. THE PUB IS ALMOST NEXT TO THREE OAKS HALT ON THE HASTINGS TO ASHFORD RAILWAY. **PARKING:** IN THE PUB CAR PARK, PREFERABLY WITH PERMISSION.

For this walk we are deep in what the Tourist Board have labelled 1066 Country, and indeed the first part of the route follows a link path between Hastings and the '1066 Country Walk', a long distance walkers' route between Eastbourne and Rye. The highlight of this easy stroll is a wander along the quiet and secluded valley of the Sailor's Stream, a tributary of the River Brede. Enjoy it while you can because this tranquillity will be destroyed if a planned Hastings bypass comes to fruition. The new road would slice across the valley leaving the footpath to burrow through a tunnel beneath a high embankment. The return route is partly along a quiet lane. At the time of writing the path soon after point 4 is underused and may be overgrown along the field edge beyond Little Maxfield, particularly in high summer. A road alternative is indicated on the sketch map.

The Three Oaks

Once a bustling railway hotel and before that a coaching inn, the Three Oaks is now a quiet country local. Surprisingly, the railway survives with better connections than many. From the tiny Three Oaks Halt you can still travel directly to Hastings or Ashford with its fast links via Eurostar to London and the continent! A free house, under new management, the pub offers all that any walker might need, with its spacious L-shaped bar, restaurant area, paved patio and small garden. A new menu offers a complete range of bar snacks, starters, main dishes and substantial puddings. The regular house beers will always include Harveys Sussex Ale and Morland Old Speckled Hen.

The pub is open from 12 noon to 11 pm in summer and at weekends, closed during the afternoon on winter weekdays. Telephone: 01424 813303.

The Walk

① From the pub turn left along the road. About 100 yards past Rose Cottage on the left, turn left along a roughly metalled drive providing access to a group of bungalows. Where the drive ends go ahead along a left field edge. Where the hedge on your left bends away to the left go ahead across a meadow without changing direction, dropping down to a stile. Cross the next field, walking parallel to power lines away to your left. Go through a wide gap in the hedge ahead and across a field to another gap to the right of a power pole. Head squarely across two more fields and across a bridge over the railway.

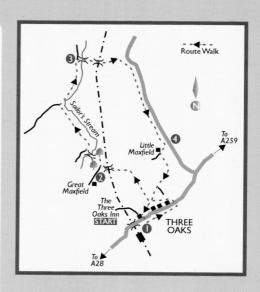

② About 40 yards beyond the railway go over a stile beside a gate and after a few yards turn right past a second stile/gate combination. A track drops obliquely down a wooded bank. At a junction, where the track becomes a metalled drive, turn right over a stile beside a gate and go ahead along the left edge of a low-lying meadow. At the far end go forward past two more gates and stiles. Walk ahead along a left field edge, over two more stiles and on between fences. Cross a footbridge and continue along the valley with a stream on your right.

③ After about ¼ mile turn right over a footbridge and climb to enter woodland.

PLACES OF INTEREST NEARBY

Hastings is within easy reach where you should make a bee-line for the **Old Town**, at the eastern end of the sea front with its narrow High Street and a group of striking black timber fishermen's huts.

Desirable residences at Great Maxfield

Cross the railway, leave the wood and bear slightly right up across a field (if ploughed and planted it may be easier to walk round the left edge). At the top left field corner skirt round to the right of a pond and walk out to a lane. Turn right.

④ After a little over ¹/₂ mile turn right along the drive to Little Maxfield. A few yards short of the farm buildings turn left through a gate and follow a right field edge. In the field corner go through a gate, bearing right along the right edge of the next field, following it left round the next field corner. Shortly go right over a stile and follow an enclosed path which skirts to the right of a garden. Once out into a field go ahead walking parallel to the right field edge. Cross your outgoing route and continue to the far field corner. Join a drive and turn left back to the pub, a few yards away.

Beckley
The Royal Oak

| MAP: OS EXPLORER 125 (GR 855240) | **WALK 28** | DISTANCE: 3 MILES |

DIRECTIONS TO START: BECKLEY IS ON THE B2088 LINKING THE A28 FROM HASTINGS AND THE A268 FROM RYE. THE PUB IS ABOUT ¼ MILE FROM THE A268/B2088 JUNCTION.
PARKING: YOU MAY USE THE PUB CAR PARK WHILE ON THE WALK IF ALSO PATRONISING THE PUB.

The highlight of this easy level walk is a stroll through the 90 acre nature reserve of Flatropers Wood. This area has been preserved and managed by the Sussex Wildlife Trust as a typical East Sussex woodland, used in the past to produce timber from a variety of trees, including birch, oak and sweet chestnut coppice as well as stands of beech and pine. It is now also the home to wild boar though you will be lucky to see

one. They are shy creatures but can get aggressive, particularly if worried by dogs when they have young to protect. Most of the rest of the walk is also within woodland including a link through the Forestry Commission area of Bixley Wood. Some of the paths used are permissive rather than rights of way and not all are marked on the Explorer map, particularly the elaborate network of paths within the nature reserve.

The Royal Oak Inn

This friendly family run pub offers a particularly warm welcome to walkers. The original hostelry dates from 1680, incorporated in the present building as a dining area and games room at the rear, both with inglenook fireplaces. The large open plan bar area at the front is a later addition but, nevertheless, over 150 years old. It is strikingly decorated with a fascinating collection of paintings, equipment and memorabilia on the theme of fire-fighting, reflecting the landlord's previous profession. Behind the pub is a pleasant sheltered garden. The beer on offer is Harveys Sussex Ale plus a regularly changed guest beer. The large traditional pub menu offers a wide enough choice to satisfy most tastes, and includes two of my own favourites, cottage pie and corned beef hash. Children are welcome, as are dogs who might like to meet the two friendly canine residents, Pickle and Stilton. Opening times are 12 noon to 3 pm, Monday to Friday and all day from 12 noon on Saturday and Sunday. For late arrivals, food is served all day on Sundays. Telephone: 01797 260312.

The Walk

① From the pub turn right along the B2088, signposted to Peasmarsh and Rye. Just past an estate road, Budden's Green, on your right, turn right along an enclosed path which continues along a left field edge. After another 100 yards go over a stile and follow a waymarked woodland path. At a T-junction turn right, go straight over a crossing path and

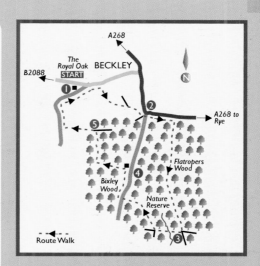

immediately, at a waypost, turn left to follow a clear path out to the A268 at its junction with Bixley Lane.

② Turn right beside this awkward stretch of road, taking care as there is no verge. After about 300 yards, just past a cottage called Oxney View on your right, turn right over a stile and follow a clear woodland path southwards, muddy underfoot in places.

③ After ⅔ mile turn right through a swing gate to enter Flatropers Wood Nature Reserve. A few yards after crossing a rustic bridge in a dip, fork

PLACES OF INTEREST NEARBY

About a mile to the north, **Great Knelle Farm** is open to the public between Easter and October. A working mixed farm of 600 acres, it offers tractor rides and animal feeding sessions for children as well as an adventure playground, woodland trail, farm shop and tearoom. Telephone: 01797 260250.

The path through Flatropers Wood

right and after a few yards, at a junction with a more substantial path, fork left. Where the main path divides, fork left, passing squarely under power lines and where it divides again, keep left (almost straight on) and walk out to Bixley Lane. Turn right.

④ Just short of the entrance to Bixley Bungalow on the left, turn left along a path which starts alongside the house and garden to your right and heads out across the Forestry Commission area of Bixley Wood. Go straight over a broad forest track. At a T-junction a few yards short of the edge of the wood turn right. Ignore a path to the right.

⑤ At the next signposted junction, go ahead over a stile. Walk along a short enclosed path to a second stile and then ahead along a left field edge with a good view to your right across the Rother valley. Ahead, you should be able to pick out the twin spires of the churches at Beckley and Northiam. A stiled path continues out to a lane. Turn right back to the start.

Pett
The Royal Oak

DIRECTIONS TO START: FROM THE A259 HASTINGS TO RYE ROAD ABOUT $2\frac{1}{2}$ MILES OUT OF HASTINGS, FORK RIGHT ALONG AN UNCLASSIFIED ROAD, SIGNPOSTED TO PETT. THE PUB IS ON THE LEFT AT THE FAR END OF THE VILLAGE. **PARKING:** IN THE PUB CAR PARK WITH PERMISSION OR ALONG THE SIDE ROAD NEXT TO THE PUB.

The Royal Military Canal was constructed between 1804 and 1806 as one of the defence lines against a threatened invasion by Napoleon. It subsequently carried some barge traffic but finally fell into disuse after 1877. Our walk follows a delightful section of the canal, now an idyllic backwater, for over a mile across flat open countryside on the edge of Romney Marsh. The return route passes through a Nature Reserve where a marshland habitat has been created from farmland under the umbrella of the Countryside Stewardship Scheme. The bird life which is now beginning to settle in the area can be viewed from a public bird hide just beyond point 3. Where the path follows the Pannel Stream keep an eye open for the kingfisher and the large blue coloured Emperor dragonfly.

The Royal Oak

Although the Royal Oak has been a pub for less than 30 years, the building is well over 200 years old and has a chequered history, having functioned at different times as private house, village schoolroom, temperance inn and shop. The pub now consists of an open plan bar with oak beamed ceiling, a large inglenook fireplace, eating areas at both ends and a large garden. The Royal Oak concentrates on providing top quality food with a large restaurant menu, including such specialities as lamb hock with mushroom sauce and Indonesian chicken curry. An impressive pudding list incorporates profiteroles and banana flambé with rum butter. At weekends you would be wise to book a table if intending to eat at the pub. During the week a simpler bar snack menu is also on offer, including ploughman's, baguettes, jacket potatoes and sandwiches.

The pub is a free house serving Harveys Sussex Bitter plus two other beers such as Badger IPA on draught. Opening times are Monday to Saturday from 11 am to 3 pm and 6 pm to 11 pm, Sundays from 12 noon to 3 pm and 6 pm to 10.30 pm. Food is served from 12 noon to 2 pm and 6.30 pm to 9 pm. Telephone: 01424 812515.

The Walk

① From the pub turn left along the main road, passing a bus shelter on your right. After about 350 yards, fork right over a stile where there is a sign 'Public footpath

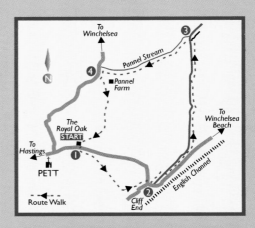

to Cliff End 1 mile'. Head out diagonally across a field to a stile and on in the same direction across two more fields, dropping down to a footbridge. Go forward across a low-lying area and another footbridge. A few yards short of a cottage go left through two gates and across the bottom of the cottage garden. Then veer half-right across a field to join a road in the far corner. Turn left and, at a junction, go ahead, signposted to Winchelsea Beach and Rye.

② A few yards past a shop on the left, turn left along a roughly metalled track, waymarked as part of the Royal Military Canal path. The disused canal is now on your right. After about 200 yards turn right over a bridge across the canal and immediately left along a path with the

PLACES OF INTEREST NEARBY

Two other excellent walking areas are within easy reach. **Guestling Wood**, owned and managed by the Woodland Trust, is just to the north of Pett and, to the south, the 600 acre **Hastings Country Park** provides a network of waymarked paths over crumbling sea cliffs and through wooded glens.

The Royal Military Canal

canal now on your left. A waymarked path now follows the canal for $1^1/_2$ miles.

③ About 20 yards short of a gate, with a tree and scrub covered cliff looming up about 150 yards ahead, go left over another canal bridge. After a few yards, go forward over a second footbridge which has lost its handrail, ignoring a third bridge to your right. Go forward along a right field edge with a stream, the Pannel Stream, on your right and the square tower of Fairlight church as a marker ahead on the distant skyline. In the field corner go over a stile to enter the Pannel Valley Nature Reserve, where there is access to a public bird hide on your left. Go forward on a wide path with the stream still on your

right and where this path veers left, go ahead over a stile beside a gate. Keep to the right of several fields beside the stream out to join a lane. Turn left.

④ Just beyond the drive to Pannel Farm on your left, go left through a gate. Follow the direction of a waymark on the gatepost squarely up across a field, over a low rise, across a stile in a dip and up to another stile on the skyline. Cross the next field, dropping down into another dip. Cross a stile and footbridge and, once out into a field corner, climb along the left field edge, until you can go left through a gate to join the access drive from a caravan site. Bear right along the drive for $^1/_4$ mile back to the pub.

Playden
The Playden Oasts

MAP: OS EXPLORER 125 (GR 918199)	**WALK 30**	DISTANCE: 2 OR 3 MILES

DIRECTIONS TO START: PLAYDEN IS A MILE NORTH OF RYE ON THE A268 TENTERDEN ROAD AND THE PUB/HOTEL IS ON THE EAST SIDE OF THE ROAD. **PARKING:** PATRONS ARE WELCOME TO PARK IN THE PUB CAR PARK WHILE ON THE WALK.

This walk is designed primarily to provide an attractive approach to the charming hilltop town of Rye, dropping down from high ground to the north into the valley of the River Tillingham. The basic walk is short enough to allow time and energy for a $\frac{1}{2}$ mile each way extension along the river into Rye, one of the original Cinque Ports, a title granted by Henry II in 1191. In 1243 it became a royal naval base as well as a flourishing seaport, though under constant attack by French raiders who, in 1377, burned most of the town to the ground. Later it became a centre for Huguenot cloth-weavers. The sea has now receded and it is a place of great charm with steep cobbled streets, many old buildings and an impressively large 12th to 14th century church. Rye is packed with tourists during the summer months but much quieter in winter, the best time for a visit.

The Playden Oasts

About 150 years old, the building was a working oast house until 1950. After falling into disuse it was converted into this unique hotel and pub about 25 years ago. The ground floor of the three circular oasts now houses a cosy bar and adjoining seating and dining areas, still with exposed red-brick walls, and there is a larger dining room in an extension at the rear. On one side of the building is a walled patio and on the other a large colourful garden. From the barrel comes the distinguished Brothers Best, alternating with Pett Progress, both produced locally by the Old Forge mini-brewery, next to the Two Sawyers pub in Pett and just along the road from the Royal Oak featured in Walk 29. The regularly changed and augmented menu offers some pretty solid fare including steak and kidney pudding and Cumberland sausage with egg and chips. There is also a full range of bar snacks (baguettes, ploughman's, jacket potatoes and French sticks with salad).

The opening times are from 12 noon to 11 pm daily (earlier for morning coffee or even breakfast!). Children and dogs are welcome. Telephone: 01797 223502.

② After another 100 yards, go left again through a swing gate and ahead along the left edge of close-cropped sheep pasture. In the field corner go over a stile at a splendid viewpoint overlooking the Tillingham valley with the river, at the foot of the hill, curving towards the hilltop town of Rye, also in clear view, crowned by its solid square-towered church. Drop downhill on a clear path with Rye now directly ahead. At the bottom of the hill, pass to the right of a large red-brick house to join a drive over a stile.

The Walk

① From the pub turn left beside the main road where there is an excellent segregated path. Where the road levels out turn right along Leasam Lane. After a little over ¹/₄ mile, where the lane divides, fork left.

PLACES OF INTEREST NEARBY

The twin Cinque Port of **Winchelsea**, 3 miles to the south, is much quieter than Rye but with equally rich historical associations. Allow time to visit the 14th century church and, nearby, the small Court Hall Museum, open April to September, mornings and afternoons on weekdays, afternoon only on Sundays.

The Tillinghham valley

To visit Rye, fork right here past a waypost indicating that you are on part of the High Weald Landscape Trail. Join and follow the Tillingham river bank, then go ahead along a road to a junction with the B2089 and turn left into the town. Return the same way.

③ To complete the walk without visiting Rye, go ahead along the drive from the red-brick house. Just short of a gate, turn left up a flight of steps in a steep grassy bank and go on up the hill with a fence, right. In the field corner go through a kissing gate into Rye Cemetery. Veer slightly right and after a few yards go ahead along a gravel path. After passing between two chapels bear right and left along the cemetery access drive and follow it out to the A268.

④ Turn right and, after 10 yards, go left along Saltcote Lane. After another 100 yards fork left along a narrower lane. Just short of a gateway flanked by two brick gateposts, fork left along a hedged path which soon drops down, squeezing between gardens, to join an estate road. Cross the road, follow a narrow path, almost opposite, and shortly go forward along the shady right-hand edge of a meadow, gently up to another swing gate.

⑤ Turn left along a roughly made up access drive. After 60 yards go right through a gate and left along a field edge, then forward along a narrow path between fence and hedge and on through Playden churchyard out to the A268. Turn right back to the pub.